USTINOV AT LARGE

Peter Ustinov

USTINOV
AT LARGE

Michael O'Mara Books Limited

Published in paperback in 1992 in Great Britain
by Michael O'Mara Books Limited
9 Lion Yard, Tremadoc Road, London SW4 7NQ

First published in book form in Great Britain
by Michael O'Mara Books Limited, London

A CIP catalogue record for this book is available
from the British Library

ISBN 1-85479-132-X
Typeset by Florencetype Limited,
Kewstoke, Avon
Printed and bound in England by
Cox and Wyman, Reading

Foreword

I have never kept a diary. The process of so doing is too rigorous for my way of life, and I know by instinct that the daily chore could never be habit-forming in my case.

Then, out of the blue, came the invitation to join the crew of a virgin newspaper called the *European*, fulfilling a growing need on this ancient continent of ours, so rich in tradition and stupidity, in genius and in waywardness, brimful of old enmities to the point of having no alternative to reconciliation and co-operation. Here was the only way I could possibly seem to be keeping a diary. A subject a week for the last year and a bit, with an immediate acceptance of the discipline, and a growing joy in the possibility of ventilating opinion.

After many months, I can truthfully say that I stand by what I have said, and agree with myself wholeheartedly throughout. To those who might say that my prediction that the war in the Gulf would be a long one was erroneous, I would answer that, despite the victory parades, it is not over yet. Not by a long chalk.

However, let the articles speak for themselves. Remember, they had only foresight to guide them, and we all know how treacherous that can be. I am willing to be judged by hindsight, and only hope you derive a fraction of the pleasure in reading this collection as I had in spilling my organized thoughts onto paper week by week.

P.U.
July 1991

Playing to the Gallery

It is not unusual in this day and age for there to be stepping stones into the world of politics other than those of the legal profession. At the time of the French Revolution, the leaders were all lawyers, from the incorruptible Robespierre to the people's friend Danton who spelt his name D'Anton before nobility became a dirty word.

Even then, one of the original bigwigs was an actor, but he was not much good at the part of a lawyer and lost his head, thereby leaving hardly a trace on the battered pages of history.

Since then, there has been Ronald Reagan whose instinctive sense of public relations carried him through many turbulent waters in which he often seemed chillingly out of his depth. In retrospect, his incumbency is remembered by those outside the United States as one long talk show, with events like Irangate as commercial breaks in which it was decided who washed whiter and who washed whitest of all.

Now along comes actress Glenda Jackson, by far the most histrionically gifted of those tempted by the political market place, who has just been selected as a hopeful for the British Parliament. I once said that those who reach the top are too often those without the qualifications to detain them at the bottom. This does not apply to Glenda who has scaled her chosen heights only now to tackle another ascent.

One thing is certain: she has it in her to become La Pasionaria of British politics. She has already displayed great qualities of intensity and lucidity on the boards. Can she now apply these gifts under conditions in which not only is she compelled to be the author of her own words, but stand before a public which is much less respectful than the one she is used to? As an actress, the theatre can ill afford to lose her immense talent. At the same time, if she is successful, Parliament can do with her technique and ability to make herself understood.

The example of Melina Mercouri is, of course, fresh in every memory. For a long period Minister of Culture in her native Greece, she is, for the moment, without a job worthy of her qualifications. I found her in Athens as charismatic as ever, but clearly frustrated by inactivity. Every conversation drifts off into politics, but this is natural in a country which practised democracy long before it found a name for it.

In Melina's case, this form of public life has taken precedence over entertainment, and understandably so. By virtue of her ability to convince, she became more of a statesman than a mere minister, a symbol of her country, known and appreciated abroad. God help the Minister of Culture who has to follow her.

Glenda is made of stuff as stern and as engaging. Perhaps the Parliament of the World will become the real arena for women's emancipation in which sheer quality will make us all forget the alleged war between the sexes.

Both Jane Fonda and Shirley Maclaine could have made the same mark in their own country if they had not shown that spark of non-conformist genius which is anathema to a nation in which candidates must pay lip service to conformity. The popularity of Mr Reagan is also evidence of the dangers of individuality and intellectual power in high places. Mr Bush has solved the problem by saying as little as possible.

Yet this is the very moment at which Miss Jackson is enjoying a triumph in the role of Mother Courage in Glasgow, currently Europe's City of Culture. She is convinced that both careers can be reconciled. But it will be hard to explain that Lady Macbeth is unable to sleepwalk tonight because the division bell in the Commons has sounded, or ask, rather nervously, if there is a Whip in the house.

To do either job well will entail sacrifice and it may be that, like Melina, the open-ended possibilities of public life will make the theatre seem claustrophobic and even inessential. But can Glenda Jackson, if successful at the start of her perilous ascendancy, help put an end to inter-party wrangling which has brought tedium and predictability to the proceedings?

Or will her talents be wasted in an auditorium the wrong shape, which occasionally erupts into party turns or, at least, turns along party lines?

11 May 1990

The World in Transit

It is a cliché to say that the world is shrinking. One of the factors which brings the illusion of sudden intimacy to this planet of ours is air travel. When all goes well, that is! When all goes wrong, we are at once with Chaucer, halted by floods on the road to Canterbury, and the world seems vast and undiscovered.

In the nature of things, airports are growing larger all the time amid a welter of apologies for the discomfort and claims that works have been undertaken for the eventual convenience of the traveller. This is nonsense, of course, since the plans for most airports were never far-sighted enough in the first place and practically every airport in the world is hastily improvising to keep in step with developments.

I say 'step' advisedly, since the moving carpets are often stopped for maintenance and the enormous distances of a modern terminal sometimes have to be covered on foot, although I have noticed a huge increase in the incidence of people being propelled to the doors of aircraft in wheelchairs only to spring out with bewildering nimbleness to take their seats.

I must say I admire the gall of these hardened travellers, even if I would find it shameful to pose as one stricken by infirmity so long as I could still struggle the full distance under my own steam – on all fours if necessary.

There has been a great increase in the number of trolleys worldwide, which is a blessing, even if some airports, notably a few in Germany and Belgium, make you pay for them in local change. What an absurd scheme for covering the initial cost of the things! Who

has small coins of a foreign country in his pocket when he sets out on a journey? Banks steadfastly refuse to accept anything but paper money, so you are condemned to useless delays at the outset of your visit, making all the protestations of a warm welcome seem hollow.

The trolleys themselves look like reject designs for Blériot's plane which first crossed the Channel. In America these devices can only be pulled which makes it practically impossible to keep your eye on your baggage as you haul it through milling crowds. In England they have brakes which you are advised to use on a gradient. I have witnessed several disasters, invariably concerning old ladies who have temporarily lost control of their vehicles while pushing them manfully up to another level or engaging in an hysterical slalom down towards the street.

Other countries boast other designs, each more wilful and erratic than the others. It is amazing how, in an epoch of growing mechanical sophistication, these primitive travellers' aids retain extraordinary degrees of perversity.

Whereas the past was full of unadorned class consciousness – first, second and third classes on trains being notable examples – no attempt was made to draw attention away from the poverty of some, the wealth of others and the thrift or social aspirations of a third group. Nowadays, the goblins of foolproof marketing have been abroad, giving us Club and European, Coach and Executive; a rich array of fancy soubriquets suggesting both that you are being cosseted, regardless of the cost, and taking advantage of a unique bargain.

Whatever class is involved in this endless masquerade, the seats are invariably too narrow for comfort and the tray touches the body of anyone with even the most discreet tendency towards corpulence.

This makes the eating of anything doused in gravy extremely speculative since whatever it is must be cut out of sight, somewhere beneath the multitude of chins which develop embarrassingly under these conditions. I make it a rule to travel wearing one of the ties I bought in India on which the extravagance of the design is merely amplified and not spoiled by stains.

The world may indeed have shrunk, but consistent efforts are being made to make it seem large after all – a place in which technique and knowledge are used tirelessly to tempt a wayward providence.

In the words of a stewardess on the London-Manchester flight: 'In the unlikely eventuality of a landing on water . . .' It would take a damned good pilot to pull that one off; or one with absolutely no sense of direction.

18 May 1990

When Time is too Short

In a rough-and-tumble world of continual technical advice, it is all a question of priorities. There just isn't time to settle every question, to argue out every fine point. Take the debate about the sanctity of life. The amount of passion spent on the subject of whether an embryo at its first twinge can be considered a human being, or whether the woman has a voice in the processes of her own little factory to the point of ridding herself of a momentary inconvenience, has brought out crowds and banners and abuse all over those parts of the world with time to spare for such contention.

A fair mind can understand both points of view, but it may also reflect that the same concern is rarely shown to children once they are born and have discernible personalities. For instance, it is now technically possible for Unicef to innoculate all the children in the world against the six killer diseases which afflict the young. The cost of this operation, officially calculated, would be the price of three sophisticated fighter aircraft.

When there is an accident at some air display in which three such aircraft are destroyed, the facts are tragic in themselves, because of the loss of life. Add to that the image of all the serum, all the vaccine in the world being gratuitously splashed over the landscape and the tragedy acquires a quality of obscenity.

Are young lives any less sacrosanct than embryos? It is all a question of priorities.

We remember how the men in the dock at Nuremberg were brought to trial when the horrors they perpetrated were still fresh in the mind. A legal procedure had to be invented gratuitously and retrospectively to accommodate the judicial systems of UK, France, the Soviet Union and the USA.

When this amalgam had been achieved, to the satisfaction of the victors at least, those culpable of the most heinous of crimes against humanity were hanged with all the melancholy pomp attached to such rituals.

Today, highly reputable politicians speak with a kind of abstract attachment about the nuclear deterrent, as though it were a basically friendly dog of war which achieved dangerous characteristics only when released, and indeed, aimed.

NATO, it is felt, should embrace both the Germanys, even before its character has altered into something more pacific and reflective of European unity. And undoubtedly a certain number of close-range nuclear weapons should be deployed on German soil, aimed at no one in particular, but able to reach into the Soviet Union.

When Hans-Dietrich Genscher says that his vision is one of a nuclear-free Germany, Western politicians emphasize that there is no hurry and suggest that there will be plenty of time to twist Genscher's arm in camera.

This only proves that politicians are consistently slower than the public they represent in giving credence to a change of mood. The disaster of Chernobyl caused universal distress, and it is difficult for anyone in his right mind to countenance a deliberate effort by any party, however righteous, to kill on an industrial scale, to throw poison to the winds and to the tides to be deposited arbitrarily all the way to the ends of the earth.

Yet that is what the nuclear deterrent is. An uncontrollable series of deliberate Chernobyls that are not the result of a tragic mistake but an instrument of policy.

So that there is no moral embarrassment as there was at the compromise of Nuremberg, one aspect of the present situation has to be clarified irrefutably before any possibility of war exists. Whoever is responsible for releasing the first nuclear weapon is guilty of a crime against humanity which makes the men at Nuremberg look like juvenile delinquents by comparison.

There is, of course, no conceivable punishment for such a criminal. But there has to be a warning to those in the habit of using nuclear warheads as worry-beads and who talk glibly of the nuclear deterrent. It is, as I mentioned before, a question of priorities. Is the sanctity of life an exclusive prerogative of the unborn?

25 May 1990

Conscience or Calamity?

The British Conservative politician, Mr Michael Heseltine, made a speech the other day based on a leaked copy of the Labour Party manifesto that had not yet been published. This caused a predictable uproar in some quarters. There is never a shortage of people who seem to detect a decline in standards, and thank God for them. For once I find myself in agreement.

The word democracy has been used and abused beyond belief. First of all it was used by the Greeks to describe what they were doing naturally and to lend some rules to a national penchant for argument. Then it was applied to the Icelandic parliament which shouted from rock to rock across a crevice separating government from opposition. Not a bad idea.

Magna Carta, the French Revolution, Tom Paine and the American rediscovery of democracy followed, and finally the word was used and abused as a way of describing every repressive government in the world, such as the German Democratic Republic and the Democratic Republic of North Korea.

Now it seems to have regained a little of its pristine dignity, but it has too often been used to legitimize a certain moral chaos. Back in the days of Watergate, high standards were still insisted upon. This philosophy led to the impeachment of a President and the condemnation of party political in-fighting.

With Irangate the rules of conduct were not as strictly enforced, perhaps because it was an international scandal not confined to mere burglary. Still, the impression left was that the rules of conduct were less stringently applied than during Watergate.

Amnesia was put forward as an alibi. Now, not for the first time, comes a leak over which the beneficiary is actually gloating and attempting to make capital.

I am not for one moment pointing a finger at Mr Heseltine, any more than I have ever castigated the profiteers from the multitude of leaks that periodically dribble out of allegedly watertight security. But I am mildly surprised that a man of Mr Heseltine's evident intelligence and political sense should still regard a leaked government document as one of the spoils of war, to be exploited gloatingly and without any sign of remorse.

Does this attitude indicate that we have matured since Watergate, or merely that we have sunk further into the abyss of cynicism? Has the leak become a legitimate outlet for expression of political policy, like deliberate disinformation and other tricks that have lost their dirtiness by the endless erosion of hands that looked clean to start with?

Industrial espionage is one of the accepted but unacceptable scourges of the manufacturing world. Politicians and the judiciary are under constant pressure as wrongful arrests and dubious sentences make justice seem not only deaf and blind but dumb as well.

Every organized society seems prone to an undercurrent of political pollution, of tremors under the soil, surfacing here and there despite concentrated efforts by the arbiters of opinion to keep such upheavals under control. Are we so far gone down the road towards a general vandalization of our principles that our societies are already beyond redemption?

Not necessarily. The European public is already emotionally ahead of the politicians. There is general disenchantment with the bickering, back-biting side of political conflict, deemed to be as predictable as it is boring and artificial.

The turn-out at elections throughout Europe is

endlessly disappointing. The battles along party lines are as tedious as the great pitched battles of history. People have their lives to lead. Their enemies are no longer each other but the elements in nature that affect their peace of mind.

So Mr Heseltine seizes on a leaked document to deliver an exultant speech full of bite and self-assurance. At the end of the day, who cares? Is that not the best revenge on those who waste our time? Is that not the best way to begin a spring-clean? And is not a blank vote also an expression of opinion?

It is up to the politicians to rekindle our interest if democracy is ever to become a way of European life again.

1 June 1990

Season for Jingoism

We are approaching the silly season during which, in the bad old days, officers of General Staffs began eyeing the frontiers. It took many wars of growing intensity and diminishing glamour to liberate our sensibilities from this sinister habit. We stood in reverence before the cenotaphs thinking of the glorious dead, the lost youth, the lost educations, the lost personalities – lost thanks to the bestial stupidity of the living.

Now a great deal has changed, even if certain instincts still lurk under the skin. The silly season no longer boasts men in boaters clinging unsteadily to railway carriages marked 'à Berlin' or 'Nach Paris'. Nowadays, a voluntary selection of manhood's flower descends like a plague on foreign cities, not as an occupying army but as loutish commandos.

Our country, right or wrong, is a creed elementary enough and rash enough to be adopted by the simple-minded, the potential killers and mutilators of society's febrile and twilit edges.

And yet, even if there is occasional havoc after football matches, let us be thankful that sport is only a substitute for war and is not war itself.

Sport may well be the embodiment of an incipient Greek ideal to the actual participants, but to the onlooker its appeal is something different. It is at once a spectacle which glorifies the ever rising limits to which the human mind and body can be pressed in the quest of athletic prowess and, on another level, it is a more cultivated form of that sacred arrogance responsible for most of mankind's greater follies.

The World Cup in Italy will, like its predecessors, be

a wonderful orgy of clashing machismos, an unrestrained outburst of all those traits in human nature now only talked about in whispers by all except bigots and members of nutty underground movements – those who defile monuments and write on walls.

Behind the sheer exhilaration of the sport itself are all the ancillary activities, the lighting of bonfires, the crackle of fireworks, the shower of objects on to the fields. Afterwards come the rampage and the celebrations, with victory and defeat losing their identity in fumes of alcohol and the weird cacophony of male voice choirs.

As a good preparation for the joys and perils to come, there are the festivals of tennis at Roland Garros in Paris and Wimbledon in London, covered by national television and some satellite channels.

If there should be any doubt about the claim that sport is a civilised substitute for war, listen to the commentaries by French, German and British experts. Should Yannick Noah or Henri Leconte be involved, the eavesdropper on a French coverage feels he is in the corner of a specific boxer rather than watching from the ringside. Since both Noah and Leconte are blessed with extremely mobile faces, the French commentators read endless nuances into the Greek tragedy mask of Noah, with its frame of wild hair, or into Henri Leconte's occasional malevolent glances.

Their description of what we can see with our own eyes is charged with private jokes, hit-or-miss sparkle and a habit of getting Czechs, Yugoslavs and Russians hopelessly muddled, to say nothing of Peruvians, Argentinians and Chileans. Switch to a German channel and there are rather fewer inside jokes. No jokes at all, in fact. Just rather weighty bonhomie which wears thin when Becker or Graf enter the lists. The muddle with Eastern Europeans and Latin Americans is the only common denominator with the French version.

The British, on the whole, give the viewers credit for having eyes in their heads and, therefore, talk rather less than their colleagues from other lands. Also, the British have the enormous advantage of having no one to root for after the first round. This puts a brake on their jingoism and enables them to avoid ridicule.

Even so, there seems to be an echo of vanishing empires in dear Dan Maskell's voice as he mutters at the sight of a British player netting a second service: 'That could prove to be a very expensive point indeed.' All in all, whichever way you look at it, there's no business like chauvinist business.

8 June 1990

Clutching at Straws

Politics has frequently been described as the art of the possible. Why, then, does it often seem so far removed from life? Take two recent events. The first is from life. A newspaper report described a drowning child watched by a group of adults on land who made no effort whatsoever to intervene, apart from one who took a safer initiative by going in search of a policeman.

That report was calculated to awaken a sense of disgust in normally constituted people.

The second example is also very much from life, but inevitably, by virtue of its dimension, enters the sphere of political reality. I refer to the United Nations' report on the threatening consequences of the Greenhouse effect.

Just when you think that Britain's Prime Minister has hardened into a mould of self-generated conditional reflexes, she surprises. Her mind is a questing one with an enviable grasp of many subjects, even if she tends to pontificate about the justness of her conclusions.

Recently she has been doing her homework and realizes the growing weight of ecologically motivated opinion among the electorate, most especially the young. So, suddenly, and practically without warning, she trumpets the alarm thereby echoing the opinion of men of science.

So far so good. We are, unexpectedly, in the realm of life. Then politics rears its inevitable head.

Britain will play her part in tackling the problems of toxic waste, acid rain and breaches in the ozone layer, on condition that other countries are prepared to join them.

Is it possible to lay down such a condition by which the future of the planet is even distantly threatened? Consider these facts and the scenario of the drowning child.

One of the onlookers has declared a readiness to wade into the treacherous water, but only if the others do likewise. The others are thrown into a discreet confusion, feeling their initiative has been pre-empted in a cavalier fashion.

One by one they make their contributions to the great political debate. One says that the water can be entered at any time but that it would be more prudent to await a full report on the prevailing tides and currents in these parts. After all, one casualty is bad enough but a recurrence of this tragic event must be avoided at all costs. 'Think of future generations,' the orator adds, with unconscious irony.

The second speaker agrees in principle with everything that has been said but insists that, because of the urgency of the matter, it is essential to refer all findings to a specially formed sub-committee.

Perhaps it will even be expedient to mobilize a special task-force to enter into action at the moment a drowning child's cries for help are heard, without having to set in motion the cumbersome machinery of bureaucracy. While this meets with general approval, some insist that it is premature and that a matter of such importance should be approached step by step.

One hothead, from a part of the world not known for its clemency, declares that there should be a way of ascertaining the political and religious beliefs of a struggling swimmer before deciding whether a rescue is warranted. This is generally ignored or roughly handled by speakers who imagine they stand on a higher rung of civilization's ladder.

All it succeeds in doing is wasting time. And meanwhile the child is drowning. In their wisdom, the

onlookers form a sub-committee and agree to convene
at a not-too-distant date in order to carry the possibility
of organizing a rescue a step further.

In due course they meet again to hear an interim
report and to be able to answer the questions of those
opposed to their policies. Unfortunately, they have to
find a new meeting place since the land on which they
had been onlookers has been reclaimed by the water.
The level is still rising.

Of the child there is of course no sign. The art of the
possible? You cannot put a market value on principles,
nor will urgency take kindly to plea-bargaining.

Either our planet is in peril, or it is not.

15 June 1990

Ping-pong at the Polls

It has become self-evident that education is the most urgent of priorities as far as mankind is concerned, apart from survival itself. There have been elections in the developing world in which the votes are counted by the number of ping-pong balls in various baskets. The access to the opposition baskets is by an aperture too small to let a ball through. Only the government aperture is large enough to receive a ball. This ingenious system leads to landslide victories for incumbent governments who call the elections in order to prove the democratic basis of their thinking.

In fact there can be no real democracy without literacy. Choice is a considered process, not one in which the mature reflection of the individual can be substituted by featuring photographs of government candidates in colour or unflattering ones in black and white of opposition candidates, nor, indeed, by apertures of various sizes.

But even in those parts of the world which are moderately literate there are frequent reversions to attitudes from which the most advanced societies were liberated centuries ago. These attitudes are often frightening reminders of our savage origins, often inadequately covered by the veneer of civilisation.

The miners of Romania, for example, are the hounds of the human manhunt, kept in kennels against the rainy day and released by leaders who then deplore their excesses later, in a manner described as 'civilized' by a political opponent whose house had been sacked.

Organized crowds are possible anywhere. One remembers the difficulty of segregating genuine poll-tax protesters from highly coherent groups of rowdies in the UK. But the fact remains that in a country like Romania, relatively backward by European standards, it is easier for unscrupulous elements to function.

One of the most subtly shocking heritages of the Ceaucescu period was the revelation that those in charge of the insanitary ghettos for orphaned and backward children were not professional nursing staff but outcasts from society, convicted of petty misdemeanours.

They had no qualifications whatever, apart from their training as pariahs. This they were able to pass on faithfully to their charges. A Romanian peasant woman, interviewed on television, thought it a good idea that all the human wreckage should be dumped together in this way. This attitude is medieval and denotes a lack of education which is quite separate from mere illiteracy.

One notices the same reactions towards paraplegics in Moscow. Their appearance on public transport is greeted with the same kind of superstitious horror that a leper might have inspired in the Middle Ages.

There have been cases of handicapped people brutally ejected from buses and I have heard, with my own ears, comments suggesting that those forced to travel in wheelchairs are, in some way, exposing their infirmities indecently to public scrutiny.

The only section of a public hospital dedicated to paraplegics in the Moscow region has just been closed. The regulations state that a hospital cannot continue to exist if another one is to replace it. The trick here is that the new one is only in the planning stage, but this is apparently sufficient reason to destroy the old one. Nobody is sure what happened to the inmates.

They were an inspiring lot since the nurses were invariably those patients who had made some progress with their therapy. They were either silent and morose, or else tumultuously garrulous. They felt deeply their social ostracism and resented it in the name of that humanity they had never known.

The most moving moment came when I reported to them the saga of Stephen Hawking who triumphed over motor-neurone disease and wrote the best-selling *A Brief History of Time*. When I recounted the story of his extraordinary triumph in the face of adversity, their eyes gleamed with a sense of wonder and one man volunteered the opinion that it was a compliment to the society in which such brilliance could flourish.

'Before we look to the future with new hope,' stammered another, 'let us thank our matron who has been a mother to us all, under the most adverse of conditions.' Matron promptly broke into floods of tears. With the great untapped store of compassion and remorse locked in Russia's Dostoyevskian heart, education to the realities of the hour is not impossible. Not impossible anywhere.

22 June 1990

Freaks of High Speed

Consider for the moment the extraordinary strain under which the human metabolism has been placed by the march of science. Take the eye, for example. Before the invention of artificial light, the working day was much shorter. Daylight was as precious as drinking water. Monks would burn the midnight oil and their eyes had to become accustomed to the flickering of lamps sensitive to every draught in the cell. Fire in some form or other was the only source of illumination once the sun had set.

During the day, the eye had no particular challenges apart from the teasing flight of birds or arrows and the usual pranks of nature – fog, hailstorms and the like. With gas came a steadier light and, finally, electricity brought an intensity which would have blinded the medieval cleric, struggling to illuminate a single letter in the gloom of his cloister.

Today it has to be asked if the eye has not met an unequal challenge imposed by the sheer velocity of moving objects of all kinds, from supersonic aircraft to tennis balls.

My first commercial Paris to London flight across the Channel in the late thirties was a journey of just over four hours and I sat rivetted in a huge club chair of wrinkled leather.

I alternated between staring at the Channel, which seemed within touching distance, and at a speedometer in the cabin. The needle wobbled drunkenly between 80 and 90mph. Even on the ground that was a considerable and dangerous speed in view of the brakes and suspensions then in use.

These days, to amplify our sensations, television installs cameras in selected racing cars and we are hurtled round the circuits in spirit, missing obstacles and other cars by inches. The emotions are not of the same order as they are on the scenic railway because it is merely a proxy participation. We also do not have the added responsibility of a steering wheel in our hands. What it does do, however, is to show us dispassionately what it is like to travel at extremely high speeds on curving roads, and it somehow explains why so many of today's accidents are attributable to human error.

The time of crisis in the field of human reaction is even more marked in spectator sports in which misjudgements are luckily not usually fatal. With modern equipment, the game of tennis has changed fundamentally from the gentle extension of the garden party to the highly organized activity it has become today.

Since the speed of the ball can be assessed, it makes us understand why the players appear so fragile. Small miscalculations or moments of bad luck, can occasion prolonged absences through injury as they never did in earlier times.

Injury and feigned injury on the soccer field have become weapons to discredit, or upset the concentration of, the opposition. The sight of a groaning player clutching a part of his anatomy is as usual today as the sceptical expression on the referee's face. If it is not gamesmanship or time-wasting, there is another area in which sports are affected by the sheer speed of play.

Tennis at Wimbledon employs a box which emits a baleful squeak when a serve is out. Unfortunately, this magic box has been known to howl in the course of a rally with the insistence of a baby demanding the bottle. The idea is to find a suitable substitute for the human eye in assessing the accuracy of a service at modern speeds. It seems hardly more infallible than the human eye itself.

During a recent World Cup match it was suspected that the Czechoslovak team had been robbed of a goal by a linesman waving his offside flag. Not a protest was heard, perhaps because the opponent was Italy, but also because nobody was sure they could believe their eyes. It was only when the action was repeated in slow motion on television that the spectator could prove his suspicion had been well founded.

Perhaps slow motion is the answer if we seek judgments which do not violate the truth. In sport, that is. But what about life? The computer can certainly be a means of reducing sheer velocity into something approaching the comprehensible. As for reality, the eye is ever a slow and delicate pupil – no pun intended.

29 June 1990

Shoot-out Sideshow

One of the wonderful privileges in having a column of newsprint at your disposal is that it enables you to make suggestions. These suggestions, far from disappearing forever into a small box displayed for that purpose in mediocre hotels, are spread over thousands of pages, provoking reactions from some of those who think they know better and positively all of those who know they know better.

Well come on then Ustinov, make use of your privilege while you still have it. Write brazenly about something of which your personal experience is confined to the mists in the outer reaches of recollection. Football.

Is it not absurd, and woefully anti-climactic, to allow a splendid match to terminate in the abitrary lottery of shoot-outs? It is as though a great war (of the obsolete, invigorating type) were to end, not with a meeting of minds over the conference table but in a game of Russian roulette played by selected private soldiers of both sides.

For such a game to be effective it would have to be played *before* hostilities and by politicians of both sides, selected by popular suffrage for exposure to this danger. Then the game would have some meaning and millions of lives would have been saved.

On the football field we enjoy a form of warfare fought by latter-day gladiators, obeying rules either too strictly or too negligently enforced by referees who have the multiple tasks of running farther than most players are asked to, while watching every detail with an eagle eye and meting out snap decisions in which undisputed authority finally counts for more than justice.

Certainly, there is so much that is arbitrary in all this, owing to the inhuman demands of the eye, ear, stamina and temperament of referee and linesmen, that the phrase, 'the luck of the game', can be invoked frequently and pointedly. At all events, there is no way of telling, apart from an extremely thorough television coverage, whether the rapid decisions inflicted on the players are justified. And by the time conclusions are reached, the game has moved on.

Even with all its imperfections, perhaps even because of them, it remains a wonderful, popular spectacle, an amalgam of strategy, tactics, precision and lunatic improvization. How awful then to have to contemplate, at the end of extra time, this untidy little sideshow of shoot-outs which, admittedly, has an excitement of its own but is quite unworthy of the epic canvas which has preceded it. Here then comes the suggestion. Obviously it would be better if the alternative solution were incorporated in the body of the game instead of being added as an uninspired afterthought.

Why not make corners count for something in the final sum? A side which wins by one goal to nil has a clean victory but, if the result is a draw, the quantity of corners in favour of a side becomes a deciding factor. In the further event of there being an equal quantity of corner kicks, the cumulative time from the beginning of the match would become the deciding factor.

In other words, if one team achieved three corners at 10 minutes, 28 minutes and 80 minutes and the other team at 11 minutes, 29 minutes and 50 minutes, the latter would have won on aggregate. All this would be calculated on the scoreboard and would add a dimension of excitement to the frustrations of a goal-less draw.

The threat of time playing a part in the case of an undecided game would invariably cut out time-wasting tactics, at least for the team which found itself with a worse corner average at any given point of the match. The fact that the sooner corners are gained, the more points a team accumulates, would guarantee attacking attitudes rather than some of the soporific stuff we are subjected to during the 'observer' phase of a game which sometimes lasts until the final whistle.

Whatever the reactions to my suggestion, one thing is clear. No method of settling differences, in any game, is quite as silly or as profoundly unsatisfactory as the shots at goal. Whatever changes there are to be must influence the final score during the course of the game itself and not afterwards. And meanwhile, watch this space for next week's suggestion. Possibly a card for dark thoughts?

6 July 1990

Freedom's Nursery

I may be wrong. In dealing with something as tradition-ally elusive as the mysteries of Soviet politics, it is always wise to start with an admission of fallibility. Yes, I may be wrong, but I'm dead sure that Kremlinologists are a good deal more wrong for much of the time.

First of all, they treat the protagonists of the great debate in the USSR as though these were veterans of party politics instead of babies who are just learning to walk in freedom's nursery.

How can the arteries of democracy have hardened already with the labyrinth of conditioned reflexes which exist in all parliaments today? There are certain rules in all the ancient parliaments of the West – rules practi-cally without exception.

For example, as soon as the head of government gets up to speak the hackles of the opposition rise. Heckling on a modest scale begins, reaching a crescendo which guarantees that the paternalistic or maternalistic words of wisdom cannot be heard.

The time inevitably arrives when the opposition has the right to reply, or at least to question. After all, what else is democracy all about? As the leader of the oppo-sition begins a statement, the reciprocal hackles rise. There is the same difficulty in hearing the words of counter-wisdom as there had been in hearing the orig-inal. And all this is played to the accompaniment of that least musical of instruments, the gavel.

It is these patterns of behaviour which are a guaran-tee of the health of the democratic process. Or so we are told. It may be true in that, of all aspects of civilized life, they most closely resemble the boisterous outbursts

31

of school life where high spirits are so much in evidence. In many assemblies of elected representatives, the very seating arrangements are reminiscent of classrooms and it would hardly be surprising to see an occasional paper dart float drunkenly in the air before plunging to earth, or ink pellets being flicked at political opponents.

I cast no aspersion on the individual members of the various parliaments, many of whom are lucid, industrious and even brilliant members of the community, but these qualities tend to disappear in the collectivity where lower common denominators begin to take over.

Individual football hooligans can be engaging and reasonable people when interviewed away from the crowd, but they become infected with the virus of boorishness when they rejoin the herd. The same pattern is too often valid for members of parliament.

And now, all too frequently, the Kremlinologists judge the dramatic events in the Soviet Union by the traditional standards of the West.

Gorbachev is seen as an innovator, easing his way cautiously forward into a no-man's land of free expression while maintaining, at least for the time being, the monumental structures of the past. Yeltsin is a fearless iconoclast, eager to banish every vestige of gargantuan socialist planning overnight. Ligachev appears to be unwilling to leave a sinking ship unless there is tangible evidence of a lifeboat in the vicinity.

These temperamental difficulties seem to suggest to the experts that Yeltsin is a radical, Ligachev a conservative and Gorbachev a tough, yet careful, man of a sort of Soviet Centre – a centre forward, one might say.

The experts seem puzzled by the fact that these leading opponents (when not attempting to put spokes in the President's wheel) express continued confidence in his leadership.

You do not have to go far to find the reasons. They

are all strong-willed men and express the differences in their personalities rather than the attitudes of this or that party. In the high adventure which is the future of the Soviet Union under perestroika and glasnost, they are all on the same side. Reactions to speeches in their parliament are personal since there are no party lines to follow.

The ship edges forward slowly under the steadying sail of history. But the Kremlinologists will have to wait for better times before they can discuss the wasteful ploys of party politics, heckling and the jeers of the unimpressed. All that is for tomorrow, or the day after, when the precious discoveries of the hour have hardened into habit – and liberty can be taken for granted.

13 July 1990

Paradise for Insomniacs

I suppose I could call this column 'Letter from New Zealand'. For that is where I am – Wellington, to be precise, after a gigantic leap through space via Singapore, Sydney and Auckland, to say nothing of a place called Palmerston North, with no trace of Palmerston South, East or West. It is traditional to feel isolated at such a distance from one's familiar scene but, curiously enough, helped naturally by jet lag, I missed less of the great sporting events than I would have done in Europe, by virtue of the fact that alternative appointments in the middle of the night are relatively rare.

Wimbledon invariably began at about 11pm in Australia, 1am in New Zealand, and the World Cup would take over at about 6am.

I normally missed most of the news summaries because I was asleep but, every now and then, I would catch one, with Mr Mitterrand very erect, trying to look a little taller than he is, Mr Kohl attempting to appear somewhat smaller and Mrs Thatcher stooped, as though inspiration was to be found at the level of their footfall.

They were at yet another summit and so thorough was the coverage that I was, at those waking moments, as well informed as I have been anywhere else in the world.

But, if technical advances in communication have eliminated distance, there are still great differences between these beautiful islands and the European experience. First of all, it is not rare to be talked to by patriotic New Zealanders who speak with powerful

Manchester or Scottish accents. They protest that they are native sons and speak of arriving eight years ago as though it were an eternity. They also affirm categorically that they have reached their journey's end.

Nothing can ever again supplant the purity of the air and the proximity of the great outdoors. When the weather is fine, even during these so-called winter months, and while the locals complain about the cold, one can only reflect that it is good to be alive and even the most agnostic of souls must have twinges of doubt about lack of belief.

The cities of New Zealand are of human dimension and, with a population of only four million, the immensity is relatively empty. Is this then paradise, the last secret place on earth where one can play the part of Adam in the Eden which stretches to the horizon and beyond?

Alas, no. That would isolate it from the rest of toiling humanity which is not in paradise, either by temperament or conviction. There is here, as everywhere, an indefinable prejudice which is extremely bad form to express as it is in every country with pretensions to being civilized.

The other day a man shot a burglar who had entered a neighbour's home. The burglar happened to be a Maori, unemployed, with several children. The man with the gun was acquitted. A distinguished Maori lawyer was invited on to a television talk-show to be asked his opinion about the prejudice of the jury. He suggested that they were swayed by the fact that the charged man was white, his victim merely Maori, and, by his accusation of prejudice, displayed a prejudice of his own.

I have been asked so many agonized questions about whether Romanian children should be allowed to enter the country. I must say that my eyebrows were probably more eloquent than my voice. Prejudice is an indefinable weed which is at its most insidious in the greenest of lawns.

It is perhaps characteristic that in this society, so enlightened in many ways by virtue of its simplicity and its graciousness, corporal punishment in schools was finally forbidden last week. There was an outcry.

One headmaster who had recently begun chastising girls (almost exclusively seniors) said he would not abide by silly strictures. The body of a cricket umpire has recently been recovered from a ravine where it had been thrown after a bondage session, involving him and what is described as a dominatrix, proved fatal. Apparently, nobody sees the links between the news items.

I know of nobody who did not wince when they first tried a ripe Camembert. Then it becomes an acquired taste. And from there it can become an addiction. Like most things in life. Even in New Zealand.

20 July 1990

Pitfalls of Patriotism

'Patriotism, Sir, is the last refuge of the scoundrel.'
Thus spoke Dr Samuel Johnson some 200 years ago.
His remark was aimed at unscrupulous figures who
attempt to cover evil actions behind protestations of
patriotism. Cecil Rhodes reminded a disciple: 'Remember that you are an Englishman, and have therefore won
first prize in the lottery of life.' This was a sentiment
shared by many people at the time it was uttered, but
which has suffered recently as the concept of life being
merely a lottery has been discredited.

I am often asked if I 'feel English'. I fear that I would
not recognise the sentiment even if I were overwhelmed
by it. Nevertheless, England is very close to my heart. I
am more than prepared to be patriotic on its behalf so
long as this does not lower or debase any other nation or
people. This is a transition period for the concept of
patriotism. It is now the duty of every citizen to see that
its country isn't wrong or, if it is, to react accordingly.
Floods of refugees or acts of civil disobedience are the
modern manifestations of dissent.

The partisans of that older form of devotion to an
abstract cause regard their sentiments as pristine, as
though endowed with a kind of vulnerable virginity.
They tend to defend this virginity even when it is under
no discernible form of attack. The recognizable symptom of this reaction in people is an outraged solemnity,
as though blasphemies, as yet unspoken, were trem-
bling on subversive lips.

Naturally, such militantly pious attitudes invite
satire, mockery and even violence. And much of the
internal conflict of today is between these points of

view. But what is this virginity that is so irresistible to the iconoclast? Surely not the purity of the race, that piece of Nazi absurdity dramatized by scantily dressed women of impressive proportions gambolling with disci? It is too late for all that. All that can be hallowed now is the irreversible mongrelization of all races.

The British way of life, for instance, is a judicious mixture of Ancient British, Roman, Saxon, Danish and Norman ways of doing things, flavoured by many incidental condiments on the side. The magnificent language, far from being a flaunting of national purity, is evidence of massive interference and borrowings which have tempered the pliant blade of self-expression into the wonderful means of communication that it is.

The virginity, then, is an illusion. All nations, even in their essence, are amalgams, the result of a primeval jostling of tribes for better bits of territory, for water, for forests, for high places. The patriotic gleam in the eye is the result of an abstract concept, the fulfilling of some sort of human need by fantasy and make-believe.

The French often speak of Gaullism. If challenged, not even they, the masters of verbal precision, can explain to what they are referring. In the words of Mr Michel Debre, ex-Premier and great exponent of fervour while singing the Marseillaise, it is 'une certaine idée de la France'. The very phrase is an admission that words simply cannot be found for this state of mind. It elevates the eye, draws the mouth down at the corners and stiffens the back. It also prepares the brain to imagine how the General would have reacted to present circumstances. Being French, it seeks to combine a deep respect for human intelligence with a superannuated truculence; the well-trodden path with the unexplored wilderness.

All nations have their altar-pieces of the mind. These are the deeply rooted causes of human conflict and gratuitous belligerency. A return to Victorian values, as advocated for our enlightenment by an elected authority, leads straight back to Cecil Rhodes and his lottery of illusory prizes. Personally, I want no part of values such as those.

But show me a Tuscan landscape, an English village green or a Russian forest; play me a Bach cantata, a Mozart opera or a piece of New Orleans jazz; let me see a Goya or Velásquez picture, a Leonardo da Vinci doodle, a Hiroshige print: open my eye to the vast panorama of human endeavour and you'll not find another patriot like me.

Whose side am I on, anyway? The side of goodwill.

27 July 1990

Life Crying for a Voice

The Victorians held that children should be seen but not heard. Nowadays they are far too often neither seen nor heard for long. In this age of unparalleled technical accomplishment, close to 150 million children will die prematurely in the course of the next decade unless the number is reduced by the advance of science.

The tough-minded, unsentimental wholesaler's view is probably that this is nature's way of ensuring that the planet has sufficient to eat; yet curiously enough, the reduction in premature deaths also has a perceptible effect in reducing the birth rate. It has been seen that once parents can be reasonably sure of the survival of their first-born, the birth rate drops. Perhaps even more tragic than the high rate of deaths among children is the miserable condition of many of the survivors, beset as they are by malnutrition and ill health, destined to be on the defensive for the rest of their lives.

Despite the terrible eloquence of the statistics, there are probably those who still ask themselves if the World Summit for Children, set for 29 and 30 September in New York, is really worthwhile. Are there not already sufficient summits? Who is responsible for organizing such a meeting and why did they do it?

In November of 1989 the prime ministers of Canada, Pakistan and Sweden, with the presidents of Egypt, Mali and Mexico, took the initiative in calling for such a summit. Their aim: to question existing priorities by elevating the importance of children in the minds, and therefore in the actions, of all mankind.

Since then twenty-two other nations, including the United States, the Soviet Union, Great Britain, France and China, have joined a planning committee to prepare for the summit, so it must be accounted influential in global terms. Eight of the nations are African, six Asian, five from the Americas and nine from Europe.

What is the urgency of concrete decisions in favour of the world's children? Here are some salient facts emanating from the researchers of Unicef and its dynamic director-general, Jim Grant. Today, 40,000 children under the age of five die every single day in the developing countries from diseases which are, for the most part, preventable. Modern technology has made it possible to produce and deliver more than enough food to feed the world.

Despite this, malnutrition in the developing world is on the increase. The wealth of the industrialized nations is more than counteracted by the degradation of the environment, violence and drugs. The sum of money necessary per annum to prevent 50 million child deaths in the next decade is identical to that expended by nations on armaments every day. *Unreasonable*?

It is also equal to that spent by American companies on advertising cigarettes every year, and the Soviet consumer spends an equal sum on vodka every month. *Unreasonable*?

Measles kills roughly one and a half million children every year. It can be prevented by a single injection priced at about 13 cents. *Unreasonable*? Diarrhoea causes dehydration which claims some two and a half million fatalities every year. Dehydration is preventable by packages of oral rehydration salts, costing ten cents each. *Unreasonable*? Most of the one and a half million child victims of pneumonia and other respiratory infections could be cured by antibiotics, usually priced at less than $1. *Unreasonable*? The technology is there. We now need a concerted effort to diffuse it and to make sure that positive efforts are not frustrated by a lack of training among community health workers, lack of access to safe drinking water and to sanitary waste-disposal facilities.

It is a thrilling moment in which to be alive. Everywhere political structures are adapted to the urgent needs of human nature. For the first time in history, crowds have reacted, in an emergency, with the intelligence of the individual. Great changes have been registered, most of them with little or no bloodshed, changes which had engendered revolutions in the past. Now is the moment for the nations and the individual to be influenced by the general atmosphere of reconciliation, of a rediscovery of our shared humanity. Now is the moment to remember that children are the future. *Unreasonable?*

3 August 1990

Food Fraud Down Under

The manner in which the world has become cohesive, and parts of it are influenced by others, is really quite striking. It has become a cliché to say that the world has shrunk, but nothing proves it quite as elegantly as a visit to New Zealand. I am seated in a magnificent new hotel in Auckland which is supposed to be opened officially today, although it has been a functioning business for a couple of months.

If I did not know where I was, the view from my room suggests that I might be in an English-speaking country. There are two neo-Gothic churches tucked among the skyscrapers. Their clocks tell different times. It is eight o'clock on a Sunday morning. The absence of a single car on the important roads which meet under my vast window reinforces this impression of wintry Protestant austerity, the traffic lights changing colour cheerlessly for nobody's benefit.

It is only a distant hint of the sea and mountains, and the huge solitary seagulls hovering above the city, which add a slight condiment of San Francisco. But the skyscrapers could be absolutely anywhere, from Winnipeg to Harare, from Singapore to Southampton.

Press the button for room service and the lad from Tonga who answered your call yesterday has been temporarily replaced by a meticulous young lass from Munich.

The restaurant I visited last night which proclaimed itself to be Italian by every folksy artefact known to man, including plaster figures of naked athletes from ancient Rome, vaunted a menu so full of errors in elementary Italian that it awakened suspicions as to the place's authenticity.

The precipitate arrival of the owner only confirmed my doubts. He hugged me to him and kissed me on both cheeks in a manner no Italian restaurateur would ever do outside Hollywood films of the thirties.

'Welcome to my trattoria,' he cried, making it rhyme with Victoria.

The cat was out of the bag. The thick accent of the Middle East gave him away. Not even the fact that he wore his hair long and was dressed as though about to launch into a tarantella could save him.

The food, I must say, was excellent, without being particularly Italian or Lebanese, but rather what an ever growing number of guide books tactfully describe as 'Continental'.

Which brings me to the kind of influences which can have no great commercial interest behind them, influences which are unsupported by publicity but which, nevertheless, spread like little wildfires throughout the world.

It is extraordinary how many men here, even in rural communities and in places like filling stations, have pierced ears and wear minute rings in them which look as if they have been pinched from pads of office stationery.

And then there is the ever-present influence of Japanese design, as expressed through the nouvelle cuisine. In another city I was taken to a restaurant which had a high reputation. The decor might have been that of an anteroom to a New Orleans cathouse. There were no other perceptible diners during the whole length of our lunchtime presence there, which speaks highly for the local taste, never mind the reputation.

There was no menu. We were told that it was a surprise, and psychologically adjusted to the part-owner's vibrations in our presence. It can't have been a good day among the wavelengths.

The pièce de résistance was served on an immense plate and included a quail's wizened fist, a section of a hare's armpit, celery looking like abandoned outriggers seen from the air on a volcanic Polynesian beach, the sea being an unidentified red sauce which managed to have no taste whatsoever. The bill, which was delirious, was served in a hollowed-out leather-bound book.

Yes, you are never really quite sure where you are. The maid has just hammered discreetly on the door. 'Can I do your room now, or shall I come back later?' she asks. It turns out she is a native of Halifax.

Nice to hear that warm Yorkshire accent again.

10 August 1990

Fighting the Good Fight

It is a fact that the trouble-makers of our times are those countries which are living in a bygone age. The trend-setters of the developed world fight their battles in the field of economics, industry and agriculture. Their feelings of hostility are aroused by such abstractions as unfair subsidies and restrictive practices, and there's very little there to incite a mob to passion.

There are, however, nations locked temporarily in history and they are usually symbolized by their dictators. Idi Amin seemed to be influenced by Richard III and Genghis Khan. Bokassa became obsessed with Napoleon, proclaiming his arid land an empire and sitting on a gigantic golden eagle throne.

Now comes Iraq, more modern, more effective, more dangerous, personified by Saddam Hussein; and Kuwait, a state which is the property of a single family, however enlightened. The attack on Kuwait earns the condemnation of the world. The United Nations acts practically for the first time as a cohesive and an effective body, owing to the accommodation between the super powers. They had managed it at Suez, Russia and the United States condemning the invasion of Egypt, but cohesion may have come about largely because the Soviet Union had chosen that moment to march into Hungary. Now is certainly the first time in which the word 'united' is relevant, and with an unusual degree of serenity.

So, sanctions are decided and all seems set for the slow strangulation of the offending party. But then, in order to deal with a problem belonging to a bygone era, the United States reverts to the bygone era itself as a solution. Despite President Bush's declaration that the actions of Saddam Hussein were unacceptable, the United States decided to call into action that vast military machine we know all too well.

Not too long ago a disproportionate armada was flung into the Caribbean island of Grenada, described by George Shultz, the former Secretary of State, as 'a nice piece of real estate'. The pretence for intervention was tenuous to say the least. It was alleged that a Cuban workforce was preparing an airport for alien bombers. In truth, Grenada had been hawking around for an airport for decades, hoping to attract tourism. A nation cannot live by nutmeg alone. No foreign capital was attracted until Cuba volunteered to help, with the result that a people's innocence was raped by an invasion as inept as a sledge hammer used against a mosquito.

I learned from one source that an American officer in Grenada noticed that navy shells were falling short of their targets. Unable to contact the ships, he called the Pentagon from a public pay phone and asked them to inform the captains. An inordinate quantity of campaign ribbons was distributed among the victorious invaders.

Of course, that was the Reagan era. The Bush heritage began with the Panama interventions and the hunt for General Noriega. Once again, a huge posse dropped from the sky with exemplary precision, destroying more than was necessary just to be on the safe side. Now the renegade is in custody, but there are growing doubts that he will ever be brought to trial since, as a long-time employee of the Central Intelligence Agency, he may know more than he should.

Now, it is Saudi Arabia, a vast tract of desert including Mecca, the Holiest of Holies in the Moslem world. This is no problem close to home but a foreign adventure if ever there was one, in the most inflammable, the most volatile section of our planet. In the old days you could tell the good guys from the bad guys by the colour of their stetsons. Today, this is not the case.

Mr Bush made it clear that this was a conflict of good and evil. Other countries are shyly joining in. Eventually, other nice pieces of real estate, such as Vanuatu or Tonga, will be shamed into sending a rowing boat to this over-subscribed field day of high morality. An act of courage. Certainly – if it works. If it does not, it will be remembered as an act of foolhardiness, especially if it lures Israel into the fray to save American forces against an onslaught by the mercurial Saddam before the crusade is fully deployed. Meanwhile, Mr Bush takes a holiday, as he did at the time of Panama. 'Life goes on,' he says. Right. So, alas, does death.

17 August 1990

How not to be a Putt out

Life was perhaps at its most elaborate at the time of King Louis XIV. Huge wigs were worn on noble heads, cascading all the way to the small of the back. Perfume took the place of soap and water and the monarch, with commendable modesty, announced that those trying to define the State should look no further than him.

Because it was the era when even men's clothes were at their most complicated, an inordinate amount of time was taken in preparing for the rigours of the day as well as for the tranquillity of the night. Thus the curious idea of the levée was born; a word still used in court circles but which has somewhat changed in its application today. Then it was used literally to describe the rising of the king from his mattress, attended by heads of departments and aristocrats. Urgent affairs of state were discussed while the royal ablutions and dressing were in progress. Time was saved. Nowadays, clothes are much simplified, breakfast is often gulped, and the excuse of working late at the office is suitably suspect.

Today's leaders do not much care for their rare moments of privacy being invaded by embarrassing questions from largely unsympathetic inquisitors. Naturally, it happens when the leaders emerge, to be suddenly faced by some well-placed journalist, that exasperation shows on even the most controlled of faces.

French President François Mitterrand shows little other than a general distaste on his ivory mask, even at the best of times. A slight twitch of irony is sometimes allowed to enliven the corners of his mouth but one feels that, even if caught in pyjamas, his composure would remain unaffected. Mr Mitterrand follows the full tradition of Louis XIV as far as appearances go. He creates height and distance wherever he goes, even though his physical stature is not impressive. He is therefore able to look down on events from below, which is a considerable knack, and to maintain in total immobility the illusion that, even if he is not the State in these egalitarian times, no one is better placed than he to be it.

British Prime Minister Margaret Thatcher has often been caught on the hop as she leaves 10 Downing Street. The light of battle immediately inflames her eye even when the questions are innocuous, and she generally gives a great deal more than she gets, out of force of habit, in the atmosphere of exuberant bellicosity in which she functions best. Chancellor Helmut Kohl is usually as self-effacing and informal as Germany itself seeks to be these days, relying on an untrumpeted imagination and efficiency for its effect. Soviet President Mikhail Gorbachev is sometimes irritated, sometimes jocular, sometimes threatened, sometimes truculent, and yet never deflected from his chosen line of directness and objectivity.

Saddam Hussein, like the Ayatollah before him, keeps a relatively low profile in times of stress. He appears so often in rather flattering effigy that there is really little need for him to appear personally. Every time the Ayatollah appeared, feebly waving from a pile of cushions, it was like a cold wind of reality after the serene portraits carried by the crowds – and the last thing Saddam needs is a cold wind of reality.

There is only one contemporary tradition which vies in informality with the levée of old. The camera does not actually invade the privacy of the President of the United States, but it does catch him consistently in moments of embarrassment during his long hours of relaxation: when he is returning to port having failed to

MITTERAND KEEPING HIS OWN COUNSEL

reel in a fish, or while he is executing an easy putt on the golf course which he promptly misses because he is speaking of Saudi Arabia at the same time. The Americans are a great nation of sportsmen and every time Reagan admitted a 'boo-boo', his popularity soared for being a guy willing to admit an error. Similarly, every time Mr Bush misses a putt or returns fishless, Saddam and the chaos he caused is blamed and Mr Bush's powers of leadership are confirmed.

When he says 'I got to run' as he accelerates out of the range of further questions, he carries a nation's confidence and sympathy with him. He has no need for a belligerent crowd to carry aloft a photograph of him taken fifteen years ago – when he can miss an easy putt in the national interest.

24 August 1990

Etchings of Defiance

Modern graffiti are either illegible, incomprehensible or vulgar. If they happen to have been sprayed on a hard surface they seem to have been executed by the same neurotic hand, that of a disturbed pastrycook perhaps, who bestrides the world with his urgent messages.

Not so the graffiti of the past which give pause for reflection. On the Balearic island of Cabrera there is a ruined fortress, once used to house a glut of French prisoners of war at the end of Napoleon's Peninsular adventures.

These wretched men, whose fate is unknown, had an abundance of nothing except time. They passed their days and mosquito-infested nights in enforced idleness while others went on with the bitter sum of human colloquy, drowned out by the wild flatulence of gunfire. Two of these prisoners, Fleury and Grapin, spent a few hours of their captivity writing their names on the peeling walls in beautiful, precise calligraphy. I ask myself unanswered questions about their fate.

Their voices sound in my ear like those of reason, of resignation, yet of defiance. But like everything else, their simple message to us changes according to the mood of the moment.

In Tasmania, where I find myself today, the landscape is dotted with little edifices constructed either at a time when this lovely island was a penal colony, or else just afterwards. Naturally, the cosy churches and other products of what amounted to slave labour have been rendered superficially attractive by the balm of time, as though nature's hair had grown over the scars on its skin and all was now forgotten, the violence, the raw injustice, the total lack of hope.

Two groups of immigrants shared the uncertain destiny of this practically virgin territory, the original aborigines having been tactfully and silently eliminated, first by unequal combat, then by isolation to a remote island where they became extinct some 120 years ago. The two groups were, paradoxically, convicts who vegetated in an atmosphere of vicious punishment and arbitrary death, and colonists in search of freedom away from the constraints of Britain.

Britain pursued them, however, decreeing in 1826 that the government in Westminster was responsible only for convict expenditure, and all civil and judicial expenses of the colonists be met by the colony itself. As usual, it required a firm hand to sort these anomalies out. Colonel Arthur was a man with the requisite gifts. Port Arthur, the isolated laager for criminals, was named after him. A church stands there to this day. How typical of that period to force chain gangs to build not only roads and bridges but churches too, in which each brick might cry out for the redemption of their souls.

Inhuman flagellations and hangings continued, but on a diminishing scale under Arthur. Gradually the savagery eased as the divisions between the settlers and the convicts became blurred and normality took over. Threats of mutiny and revolt gave way to a change of habit and, finally, to the abandonment of the whole penitentiary system and the removal of its last element to Hobart, the capital, under lock and key in a conventional prison.

There is something solemn, an aura of unpleasantness, which hangs like a curse over places where human beings have suffered unbelievable cruelty at the hands of their own kind. The feeling is present in the greenery of Bergen-Belsen, with its cosmetic aspect of a sinister golf course. It is present in Babi-Yar, in Kiev, another scene of slaughter, where the traffic, although close, becomes inaudible. It is present at landmarks in Siberia, however caressing the sunshine and cleansing the snow. It is present in the churches built by the condemned. The sounds of wailing and of the peremptory orders of stupidity are only just out of earshot.

In these days of the high moral tone, adopted with such facility as an excuse for unspeakable acts, the nations which once scanned the horizon for a glimpse of opportunity still have a great deal to answer for. When pomp and circumstance are silenced, there remains the infinite reproach of the downtrodden, the despised and the destroyed. And there remains human resilience, the unreadiness to be bullied out of a certain elegance of the spirit. There remain, for all eternity, Messieurs Fleury and Grapin.

31 Aug 1990

Twists to the TV War

While no state of war exists, any member of a democratic society has the possibility, and indeed the obligation, to speak his mind. There is absolutely no patriotic duty to echo the more strident sentiments of the popular press, nor to take all we are told without a pinch of salt.

We all know the facts. It is perhaps time to study objectively what lies behind them. Saddam Hussein executed a swift surgical annexation of Kuwait. Owing to the recent accommodation between the superpowers, the United Nations, instead of remaining a sterile battleground, suddenly developed into the effective forum which its founding fathers had always intended. Sanctions were universally accepted as a Draconian measure to fit the crime. At this juncture the rest of the world held the initiative.

Then the United States, sole possessor of a vast arsenal of weapons, decided to enforce the UN's decisions. It did this before it had a mandate to do so, but with a feeling that it was merely forestalling the inevitable. Some countries felt that sanctions should take effect before invoking other solutions.

Everyone knows that the hawks have President George Bush's ear, at least intermittently. Dr Henry Kissinger and General Alexander Haig both feel that the United States, having come this far in military build-up, would suffer humiliation if Saddam Hussein escaped unpunished. This is a viewpoint, like any other, and its exponents have every right to express it. The talk is of tanks and warships, the possible deployment of poison gas and even nuclear weapons. The threat is of a mega-war, hopefully short.

Then comes the Iraqi counter-attack, expected to be on the same overblown level as the threat. Not at all. It is being conducted with the minimum expense and the maximum effect, and is a revolutionary move in the history of conflict.

Saddam Hussein appears in hotel rooms with the potential Western hostages, patting children on the head and speaking in measured and reasonable tones. Relatives of the detained are enraptured. One old couple regard the appearance of the progeny on the television as a 'miracle'. Others express relief and are optimistic.

A section of the Western press threatens to burst blood vessels in its paroxysms of fury. The media and politicians speak of bad taste. Even Dan Rather, the excellent correspondent of CBS television, tells Saddam Hussein to his face that the whole enterprise made him feel uneasy. Exactly as it was supposed to.

The taste is certainly not of the best, but then it

seems to be a part of a dictator's instincts to make a beeline for the babies in moments of difficulty. Saddam is no exception.

His febrile fingers never stop patting juvenile heads or lifting recalcitrant chins for the purposes of ocular contact. And when he stops for a moment, his obedient henchmen take over. No, the interviews are clumsy and disjointed but they are part of history. They have regained the initiative from the iron-clad hordes of the free world and we must recognize this fact.

That the whole ploy is in bad taste is evident, but what could be in worse taste than gratuitous death during a pre-emptive strike? President Kurt Waldheim goes to Baghdad and comes back with a plane-load of Austrian nationals. He is thoughtlessly accused of breaking Western solidarity. Since when has he, of all people, benefited from Western solidarity? As President of Austria, responsible for Austrian lives, his initiative was entirely correct and laudable.

President Bush has appointed a Mr Ailes to improve his image. Judging by a brief appearance on television, Mr Ailes may well do wonders inside America, but he is too bluff and arrogant to put the rest of the world's mind at rest. And when British Prime Minister Margaret Thatcher turns on the public, as though she has heard whispering in the dormitory after lights out, it is because she is combating the insidious effects of the Iraqis' new methods the only way she knows how – by a contained stridency.

If there is, indeed, whispering, it is because there is a great deal to whisper about, not the least of which is how to develop our own trump card without relying too heavily on the methods of the past. Television is here to stay, and not merely to entertain.

7 Sep 1990

Hotchpotch of Culture

The phrase 'multi-cultural society' is quite a new one. There has never been any call for it before because for centuries, it has not existed outside the palaces of monarchs. And in those days, even the word 'society' had a more limited and rarefied meaning. It has always been fashionable to have a decent knowledge of things foreign. French has always dominated as a language of the Court, unless it was English with a discernible German accent. Italian was the language of music, Japanese and Chinese the language of the martial arts.

But now, as the world has shrunk to size with the conquest of distance, Australia is perhaps one of the most valid arenas in which to watch the spread of multi-culturalism.

Coming here in 1960, and being a microcosmic multi-cultural society by itself, I have always been very sensitive to this tendency. In those days, Australia was a little like an England only touched remotely by wars, Gallipoli being an event of which the bungling was tactfully hidden so that the legend might live and flower. There was a certain amount of anti-oriental feeling, freely expressed. After all, a huge, under-populated land considered itself vulnerable to the teeming millions in the north searching for Lebensraum and a means of survival.

Many industrious Australians still grumble that, in the main, their fellows are an idle lot, failing to match the work-hours or the work-ethic of many underprivileged people. And here, of course, we have the root of the problem. Australians are overprivileged, especially by virtue of their climate. Winters are short and, on the whole, benevolent. The other seasons are long. There is always the temptation of sport, a means of physical exhaustion more attractive than addiction to the production line.

Last week, when it was still winter on the beaches near Melbourne, the seascape was alive with joggers and with a swimmer or two. But, of course, I sat watching this ebullient activity on the verandah of a restaurant run by a couple from the French-speaking part of Switzerland. That the Swiss should know how to cook exquisite seafood is already a cultural confusion of the first order.

Back in 1960, there was a harmless lunatic in a parody of a stormtrooper's uniform who used to goosestep to the supermarket in a small town in South Australia, singing old marching songs in a croaking voice. He was regarded as a colourful relic of the distant past.

Now Australian legal authorities are engaged in a protracted and no doubt expensive debate to decide if the prosecution of an Australian-Ukrainian in his late seventies for alleged war crimes lies within the competence of a local court. One can see that Australia is growing up, and not always for the better. It will be tragic if she loses her sense of proportion, at the moment one of the most attractive aspects of this medium-sized land of delights. There can be no witness of whatever war crimes there were who is less than seventy. Most of them are certainly dead. Only the judge will be far younger. Would we have considered it reasonable for war criminals of the First World War to have been brought to trial (I refuse to call it justice) as late as 1965?

Yet now, to give an air of solemnity to the vigil in the Gulf, a voice of high moral purpose has threatened Saddam Hussein with an eventual procedure similar to the Nuremberg trial. God help us all. Australia will, no doubt, be asked to furnish a judge because of her contribution of three ships to the blockade. And that judge, if things run to their usual schedule, is at this time at the kindergarten and doing well.

But all is not lost. A multi-cultural society suggests a wider diversity of opinion than was usual previously. Already, Arab-Australians protest against certain monolithic actions and open our eyes to different aspects of the Gulf conflict.

But does multi-culturalism not dilute the personality of a nation? Talk to the tennis players Fromberg, Stoltenberg, Kratzmann, Masur and Limberger. With names like that, they could be American – even German. One word exchanged is enough to realise that they are as Australian as 'good on you'.

And so are the fine cheeses and delicious wines, even with names such as Tasmanian Brie and Cabernet.

14 September 1990

Turning Pink of Red Tape

Bureaucracy must have had a heyday, during which the very thoroughness of the way in which information was stored seemed a model of efficiency – in much the same way as complicated drill on the parade ground was generally accepted as a symbol of military prowess on the battlefield.

Then, with the advent of the microchip and the computer, the mass of stored information and the dizzy hierarchy required for its maintenance became, gradually, the visible proof of all that is wasteful in government. For example, the West African Republic of Benin is the only one I can remember to have extracted from me the maiden name of my maternal grandmother. I hated giving the information up since I was already suspicious of the uses to which it could be put.

Over the years nothing has come of it. Evidently Benin not only discovered that little could be done with the surrendered facts, but she was also constrained to change her name from Dahomey without being able to conceal the news from bureaucrats the world over. Such gratuitous changes cost the bureaucratic establishment a great deal of money.

Think of the colossal upheavals in philately and numismatics when Ceylon decided to become Sri Lanka, Upper Volta Burkina Faso, Persia Iran and so forth.

The repercussions reverberate all the way down to the Olympic Games which require the juggling of alphabetical orders and, at times, the lightning study of new national anthems.

Sometimes, of course, a form of cynicism was

allowed to pollute the pristine arteries of mega-administration. Compelled to stand in line for a long while at the American embassy in London, I was able to reflect on this. My reason for being there was to procure a passport for my youngest daughter, then aged six weeks.

One of the items on the questionnaire was: who are your two best friends in the US? This was to be filled by either parent or guardian in the event of the inability of the recipient to fill in the form herself. I left this answer blank.

Eventually reaching the vice-consul, a powerful and somewhat masculine lady with a bass voice, I protested my inability faithfully to translate my daughter's predilection in the matter. I was told in no uncertain terms that all questions had to be answered and, while I thought about it, I lost my place in the line.

Annoyed, I put down Harry S. Truman and Senator Henry Cabot Lodge, both of whom had, on an earlier occasion, leaned over the pram and waved down at my daughter. Later, I reached the vice-consul again. She read my insert and commented, unsmiling, in her deep voice: 'Now why didn't you write that in the first place?'

I remember being asked in another document from the American administration what colour I was. Unused to such a question at that time, I thought it would be honourable to be as precise as humanly possible. With this in view, I put down 'pink'. This was the time during which communist sympathisers were referred to as 'pinkos'. I was not to know that, but I was told in no uncertain terms that I was white. I denied this hotly, declaring that I felt perfectly well.

Another category I have never got used to is Caucasian. In my narrow experience, this appellation can only describe Armenians, Georgians or Azerbaijanis, all exclusive inhabitants of that beautiful part of the world. To insist on being a Caucasian seems to my mind as out of place as declaring oneself to be an Aryan in a document emanating from the Third Reich.

Now, after more than nearly half a century of adult existence on this planet, I have begun to wonder if it matters at all what one writes on official documents. Once, forced by overcrowding to share a hotel bedroom in Limoges with my mother, I wrote on the hotel ledger that my name was Oedipus Rex and that I was a manufacturer of bathroom fittings from Liège, Belgium. There has never been any repercussion from this.

And while we're on the subject, in this epoch of glasnost and perestroika, I wish to share with the world classified information which has, up to now, only been available to the Benin government. The maiden name of my maternal grandmother was Maria Sapozhnikova. She was a Caucasian Aryan and her colour depended on the time of day. There. I've left no space unfilled.

21 September 1990

Murder in a Moral Guise

Sooner or later everyone must decide, to his own satisfaction, to what extent moral ascendancy is vital in an international conflict. Personally, I believe that no victory is worth winning without it. This is evidently also the opinion of those who believe in the Puritan ethic. It is essential to fuel the outrage inspired by the original act of violence.

However, it is inadequate to keep repeating the facts like a litany. Circumstances change during an extended crisis as the weather changes. Professionals take over – those who are compelled to work within narrow horizons, to carry out orders. I am aware of one of Mrs Thatcher's many condemnations of Iraq in which she declared that the claim that one was merely obeying orders is no longer a sufficient excuse for war crimes. Quite correct.

But then along comes General Dugan with a catalogue of war aims, expressed laconically. General Dugan, I must remind you, was the Air Force chief of staff who has since been sacked for sharing the military options with journalists. His potential targets included the obvious ones but then proceeded, with growing refinements, to 'Iraqi power systems, roads, railroads and perhaps domestic petroleum facilities – though not the oilfields'.

A nice distinction, reminding us why we are there, moral outrage aside. General Dugan, nothing if not thorough, asked his planners to interview academics, journalists and Iraqi defectors to determine 'what is unique about Iraqi culture that they put a very high value on'.

Already the war aims are becoming sleazier. After all, the planners might well argue, it is not the first time in history that Babylon has been destroyed. They have also identified three 'culturally very important' sites in Iraq – possible religious centres – which the US Air Force would avoid. That's good to know from aircraft coming in the general direction of Mecca. Apparently, Israeli sources had advised General Dugan that the best way to hurt Saddam was to target his family, his personal bodyguard and his mistress. This operation goes by the name 'Decapitation'.

Obviously, assassination by any other name is illegal if not unconstitutional. The US cannot indulge in terrorism at a time when terrorism is condemned. Things have changed since the days when a CIA man drove around all day with Patrice Lumumba's corpse in the back of his car, wondering where to dump it.

But apparently it is OK to aim at eliminating an entire entourage in the hope that the intended victim will be in its midst. This was done in the raid on Libya in which a child was killed but in which Colonel Gaddafi escaped. The bombers in that heroic adventure left from bases in Britain.

One has cause to be grateful that General Dugan's quiet outburst was quickly punished by his dismissal. But there was no indication that any of his claims were false. He was reprimanded for his indiscretion, not for fabricating information. The general's sin was not so much sabre-rattling as lifting the veil on other rattling sabres and this could well be taken as yet another signal to Saddam Hussein to be reasonable and surrender to the superior power, not of the US but of the entire world, to borrow a phrase from President Bush.

And of course the longer the crisis goes on, the more difficult it is to remember the pristine days of that unique United Nations resolution. Those in a hurry have muddied the waters. We no longer see as clearly as

66

we once did, and that is the fault of our side which has sought refuge in old-fashioned solutions like the force of arms. Smiling colonels on television, who declare that their weapons are so sophisticated that they never even see the enemy, do nothing to alleviate a sense of moral disgust at the final idiocy of such shows of strength.

Obviously the punitive expedition cannot stay in the cheerless cauldron of the desert forever, and it is too late for doubts about whether the planners ever thought their actions through to conclusions which were other than emotional. What happens next is anybody's fear. It is deeply depressing that the West is unwilling to trust sanctions and must rush to a military option. But military solutions without a constant weight of public opinion behind them are no longer obvious solutions. The battle is for the high moral ground as well as for victory.

28 September 1990

Penthouse Paradox

A curious world we live in. Rampant poverty on television, empty shelves in the Soviet Union; old ladies complaining about the state of things while politicians waste eloquence on each other and confide in asides to the Western press that whatever the solution, it is more than urgent.

Scenes of riot and rapine which the newscaster warns are worse than most viewers could possibly bear. Merciless beatings in Soweto or Monrovia, bodies on fire, lunatic creatures running forward in a stooped position, firing machine guns at nothing in particular.

Members of the Iraqi dad's army rehearsing a potential disaster with all the verve demanded by their coach. Men, women, children and gathering piles of windswept garbage, stuck hopelessly in the swirling desert, while profiteers make killings selling bottled water at the price of wine. Then, a return to another kind of reality, at the turn of a switch. The cosseted, sometimes absurd luxury of hotels engaged in ferocious competition as to which can make the most useless gestures in the direction of ultimate bliss.

For me there is no luxury which can replace that pinnacle of serenity – home. I know more or less where everything is, even if I have to walk to fetch it. The exercise, they say, is good for me. Raiding the larder is not at all the same as raiding the mini-bar. There is a tranquil disorder in my home which finds no parallel in the hoovered expanses of pile carpet or bald marble tables with stereotyped messages from the management on them. And, of course, a person watches far more television when he is on the road for three months in grand hotels, far from home.

Consequently, far more riot, revolution, malpractice, sadism and suffering than usual. And strange local newspapers shoved under the door with more expressions of goodwill from the management.

I could not help noticing that the business sections of these newspapers grow fatter and fatter to accommodate the kilometres of baleful information churned out by the ticker-tape machines. Generally, in this semblance of reality, far from the transient tragedies of television, an observer cannot fail to sense a terrifying impression of instability, as though the appearance of surpassing opulence is a mere mirage.

The market, so lauded by the apostles of monetarism, seems at times merely an arena for jugglers and mountebanks, in which huge fortunes are made and lost by the instinctive reactions of gamblers. The old idea of a capitalist as a hard-bitten manufacturer with retrogressive attitudes towards worker participation, a man of iron will who backs his own hunches to the bitter end, is as dead as mutton.

Today there are no particular qualifications attached to those with vast, if transitory fortunes. Everywhere special issues of magazines are published entitled 'The 500 richest men in the world', 'The richest men in Australia', and so on. Lists appear with the pin-point of accuracy of the taxman declaring the exact earnings of Stefan Edberg, Boris Becker, Steffi Graf and Martina Navratilova. Presumably, all this is done to stimulate public greed in a world increasingly devoted to the concept of greed as an ethic.

Unfortunately the rules of the market are enforced as rigidly as the speed limit. You'll never be stopped if you drive just a little too fast. A degree of doubtful practice will also pass unnoticed. As for the rest, it's a matter of luck.

As a rule, the prisons are over-full of minor criminals

who don't know better than to get caught – people searching desperately for the wherewithal of capitalism. If those of a certain notoriety go to jail, it is seen as an unfortunate quirk of unkind destiny and they seem more like displaced persons than jailbirds. Meanwhile the camels grow larger, the eyes of needles microscopic, and the money lenders build new temples at a profit.

And the penthouses of hotels are just the places to savour this climate of biblical paradox.

There was one enormous suite in which the floor seemed to undulate precariously, as though it had not been finished in time, and the rich carpet had been stretched over an uncertain base. This was an apt symbol of the general sensation of impermanence as the balloons of the speculators just beg to be pricked.

5 October 1990

The Mouths of Babes

So the greatest summit is over. A weekend in New York, dedicated at the highest possible level to the future of children. An extraordinary initiative, the dream of Jim Grant, the man with the wild visionary eyes and mouth like a guillotine, a boss Unicef is lucky to have at this time.

Incisive when need be, this son of a missionary will only take no for an answer if yes is to be the answer tomorrow. His fulgurant, if patient, enthusiasm proved to be contagious. Brian Mulroney of Canada and President Carlos Salinas de Gortari of Mexico were among the first infected and passed the happy plague around with selfless generosity.

Six nations brought the idea of a forum to the world's attention and soon there were twenty-two sponsors. Once the movement had attained that figure the urge turned into a fashion and the number increased to seventy-one. This unprecedented number of heads of government compelled the organisers to limit their contributions to four minutes each. A few prime ministers declined to come. They were doubtless among those more eager to talk than to listen, which is probably characteristic of their calling.

Mr Bob Hawke suggested to me that it was a long journey for four minutes on the podium and, on a ration of miles to minutes, one has to agree with him. Of course, this presupposed his willingness to abide by the rules. Mrs Thatcher, coming a shorter distance, elected to take a little longer than the statutory time, confident that no power on earth has yet been devised which is capable of curbing her oratorical flow. Her speech was judged a good one, even by those with no particular sympathy for her policies. Mr Havel of Czechoslovakia also borrowed moments of time, but then he is a poet and deserving of licence.

Cynics decided that, at its best, the summit was a gigantic ego trip for the leaders of the world, dressed in Hans Christian Andersen's Father Christmas outfits, borrowed from the emperor. It is far too early to judge if the cynics have a point. Personally, I prefer the rather healthier and more intelligent scepticism of children to the gratuitous cynicism of their elders.

We questioned various groups of children about the summit meeting while it was going on. The results were frequently surprising; there were the eight students at a New York school in a sector of the city neither privileged nor appetizing. Only one black boy knew of the terrible difficulties of the African continent. Asia and Latin America he considered not to be his concern.

The other kids were obsessed with the dramatic situation in New York. One told of a celebrated manufacturer of leisure clothing who has begun producing bullet-proof vests for schoolchildren to use in the playground. He regarded New York as a real jungle compared to the peaceful habitat of Tarzan and his chattering apes. One might have thought that the patriotic mood would have rubbed off on young people exposed to endless television and the oversimplification of facts diffused by the media.

Not a bit of it. The idea of war is out of style. The most voluble boy had three relatives already in Saudi Arabia. They were evidently linked by ties of unusual affection. 'What happens to me if they get killed?' he asked lucidly. 'It's bad for them. It's just as bad for me, on account of I stay alive, with a lot of bitterness. The adults never think of the kids when they make their decisions.' Then came the most surprising part. 'And how about them Saudi kids and the kids from

Eye-rack? I guess we got more in common with them than we got with any of our parents.'

'Do you all agree?' I asked. There was a chorus of assent. It had evidently been a subject of conversation among themselves before we asked the question. I told them that Prime Minister Mulroney had said it was up to the children to hold the politicians accountable for their good intentions and to force them into action. President Salinas even suggested a compulsory yearly progress report from participating nations.

An older girl asked if it was true that the US had not yet signed the declaration. I tactfully explained that there had been an American signature, with a proviso that the signature was not binding. 'A disgrace,' she said. 'We should have been the first.' I think that mere politicians are asking for the kind of trouble that only genuine statesmen will welcome.

12 October 90

Mr Bush is on the Ball

Walter Mitty was a charming and profound invention of the late James Thurber, a romantic daydreamer as redolent of certain traits in human nature as Don Quixote, Falstaff and the Good Soldier Schweik. One sometimes hears a complaint about a new movie or a new play, that there was no one character in the cast with whom the viewer could identify. Personally, I have always found it difficult to identify with anybody other than myself. That does not make me the best element of an audience.

Walter Mitty, on the other hand, never stops identifying himself with any character that comes along, investing him, and therefore himself, with heroic dimensions. The charm of this process lies in the illusion of notoriety imagined in the poetry of a mind relegated to a humdrum existence. If this illusion enters the world of the possible, of the prosaic, it is at once divested of all charm.

Let me explain. When I was young, the veteran King of Sweden was a potential Walter Mitty but his qualifications were rendered suspect by the fact that his social position allowed him to bring his dreams to a kind of reality. Walter Mitty would have had to imagine his ascendancy over the great tennis stars; the King of Sweden was able to play with them, and there are many photographs of him leaping to smash, his glasses glinting in the sunlight, his mouth ajar with effort, while the luminaries of the epoch, Borotra, Cochet or Lacoste stand by with perceptible but measured respect at the sight of this blue-blooded octogenarian straining to turn his dreams into a much less attractive reality.

And now, along comes Mr Bush with some of the same problems, expressed more acutely by virtue of his relative youth and startling physical condition. He has an aversion to being seen jogging. This is understandable. Jogging does not bring out the most aesthetically seductive aspects of people. In any case, it is undeniably only practice, not the three-minute mile itself.

When Mr Bush is caught at the wheel of his golf-cart, circumstances change. The ectoplasm of Walter Mitty is visible in the background, as the cornered president seems to eye an imaginary Ayrton Senna in Pole Position by his side. As the questions of journalists become harder to field, the red light changes to green with expedient haste and our hero accelerates away to beat Senna to the first corner.

If journalists have the bad taste to appear on the scene just as Mr Bush is putting to defeat Nick Faldo at the 18th hole, he manifests his irritation by missing it by so wide a margin that the observer's sense of fair play is called into contention. The look of Mr Bush, both pained and pinched as he surveys the golf course, suggests that he thinks of distant Kuwait as a vast inhospitable bunker which must be delivered from a rude fellow who doesn't even know the rules of golf and who believes that bunkers are to be coveted instead of avoided.

Perhaps it is in the nature of tennis that it is only really possible to follow in the wake of Walter Mitty in the realm of the daydream. Reality imposes its own implacable rules. Whereas golf, athletics, motor and speedboat racing involve competition between people without direct physical contact, tennis is a shared experience of a different category.

The ball is the link between the rivals and reality thereby banishes the pipedream. Senna, Faldo, Carl Lewis, even Saddam (pronounced to rhyme with Madam) can be safely imagined. Lendl, Becker and

Edberg cannot. And it's here that the process loses its charm. The president is a good enough player and a sufficiently eminent figure to solicit the presence of some leading players on his court. It is a new interpretation of the phrase, 'holding court'.

By sheer chance, I came across some of the excuses employed by stars to avoid these encounters. One celebrated gamin of scintillating achievement suggested that he would find it impossible to modify his service to accommodate the chief executive, while another player suddenly developed a tactful physical incapacity of short duration.

The youthful Pete Sampras lent himself to one of these diversions, revealed at the very moment of the first budget deadlock.

19 October 1990

Yesterday's Bogeyman

That I am inexperienced in the field of journalism is self-evident. However, I am eager and learning fast. A normally constituted greenhorn's mistake is to supply too much material in the belief that a baker's dozen is a conscientious way of fulfilling a contract. If it is too long to fit the prescribed space, however, his piece may be cut to size by having its end lopped off.

Now any storyteller will confirm that a cardinal rule of engaging attention is to leave the punch line to the last, with the result that my pieces often lead up to a conclusion which is conspicuous by its absence.

Take last week's article. It was a light-hearted speculation about the Walter Mitty-like fantasies playing on George Bush's mind and his success in luring that most promising young player, Pete Sampras, to play tennis with him. A fraction of that game was aired on television in New York on the very day the government shut down in the absence of a budget.

Perhaps you will permit me to give you the end of my piece now, before I belatedly begin another. In the section of the match which was shown to us on TV, we saw that the president and Sampras were playing on the same side of the net, without so much of a hint as to who their opponents were. Speculation was rife. Kissinger and Chang? Sununu and Krickstein? Or a couple so feeble they looked defeat in the face before the first ball entered into play?

Whatever the truth, I concluded that in this kind of game you have to keep your eye on lips or hips. And, meanwhile, crisis anyone?

This was the conclusion of the piece and it leads quite naturally to the new, very brief article.

What is the difference between intractability and flexibility, and is it the same difference as that between stupidity and intelligence? There are those who equate a desire to find a diplomatic solution to the Gulf crisis with the attitude of the appeasers before the outbreak of the Second World War.

To anyone who is old enough to have been alive during the time of the great appeasement, there is one vital difference. In those days, the establishment were the doves; today, the establishment are the hawks. Then they believed all Hitler told them and perhaps, because of the rude awakening then, they elevate Saddam Hussein to the same level of horror as yesterday's bogeyman.

The opposition to the errand of mercy by former British Prime Minister Edward Heath is typical of today's insecurity masquerading as firmness. It is always the nervous finger which fidgets in the vicinity of the trigger. Compassion is never the result of dreaded weakness but, rather, an outer manifestation of a great inner strength. Those who regard any discussion with a potential enemy as a compromise with terrorism are those who lock their intelligence in a drawer and throw away the key.

Why? Because there can be no intelligence without flexibility of mind. This does not, for a moment, mean that profound conviction should be betrayed, merely that an open mind is far more likely to have a balanced view of both doubts and convictions than a closed one. What the hawks glibly refer to as a rapid, surgical strike has never worked. Pandora's box is full of nightmarish surprises. That is the only receptable which should be kept locked and the key thrown away. All sorts of insinuations are emerging about the events leading up to this crisis. The moral issues which caused the United

Nations to vote are still clear, but the steps which led up to the crisis itself are tinged with disturbing revelations and cross-currents.

Compared to this murky imbroglio, Mr Heath's mission was clear as crystal, and not only those immediately concerned will bless him for the clarity of his vision and the real strength of his character. And here I must end; the baker's dozen in journalism being eleven words.

26 October 1990

Sunflowers for Peace

It is somehow disconcerting to realise how difficult it has been for human societies to live without enemies across the wide span of history. Just as in sport the champion needs an opponent to bring out the best in him, so the nations have required endless tests of strength and confirmation of manhood.

This, of course, lasted while war was still an activity of human dimension in which weapons were mere extensions of physical strength. Since they became inhuman, during the Great War, and, finally, unthinkable today, there has been an evident reassessment in progress, inspired by Gorbachev and emulated by all capable of mass-destruction. Naturally this has created a problem for the traditionalists, those attached to the concept of the indispensable enemy. NATO must decide what it is defending Western values against. There are those who still regard the Soviet Union as a potential foe by virtue of the sheer quantity of rusting tanks and mouldering missiles, and there is never a shortage of old-fashioned cranks like General Galtieri and Saddam Hussein who rekindle the dream of indispensable military might in others.

But these are passing phenomena. History has already sounded the death-knell of armed strength as we know it. For the time being, the military have become an endangered species, as the dodo and the pterodactyl once were, and not a moment too soon in a world lacking in nothing but feelings of general trust and fraternity. Police and anti-terrorist squads will probably always be needed, so there will always be an outlet for those with a gift for controlled belligerency.

But in the main, it has been accepted that war as an exercise in human high spirits has already been struck off the sporting calendar after millennia of wasted life.

What can replace it? With almost indecent haste, economics has taken the place of military confrontation. Of course, it can always be argued that economics lay at the base of most terrestrial aggrandisement in the past but, nowadays, it has acquired velvet gloves, especially when animated by the intelligence of the Japanese. No sooner did the colours of the Soviet Union fade from the field of human conflict than the golden chrysanthemum of Japan shone bright to irritate the quarrelsome: those who cannot stand a vacuum. Suddenly, there were allegations of unfairness, of intractability, of opaque dealings within the mysterious hierarchy of Japanese power. In fact, Japan profited greatly from her exclusion from the arms race. Her inherent ingenuity was pressed into the service of more profitable goals. And, however local her purchases, nobody can accuse her of narrow vision.

Those who bought Van Gogh's *Sunflowers* for an unprecendented sum expressed the conviction that, in view of the publicity attached to this deal, they had got away with a bit of a bargain. This is not a claim from the mean-minded. In the main arena, Japan has caused consternation in the electronics and car industries by dispensing with such ramshackle philosophies as 'built-in obsolescence', a strategy aimed at the gullibility of those purchasers eager to be 'in style' with 'state-of-the-art' gadgetry. This Japan has achieved not by imitation of the West but by producing goods of startling reliability, strength and efficiency. They don't have to build in obsolescence since technical innovation cannot always be foreseen. All that is sure is that it is on the way.

A remarkable aspect of this velvet invasion is not so much its intensity among the high-profile activities, as its scope away from the spotlight. Lucas Carton, one of the beacons of Parisian gastronomy, where that great chef Alain Senderens exercises his art, is now a college for potential Japanese chefs as well as being a restaurant in which standards have not been affected one iota. The Hotel Vier Jahreszeiten in Hamburg, always in the 'best ten' lists, is now Japanese-owned. The revered trams of the city of Melbourne are owned by the Japanese and leased back to the civic authorities. Why? Perhaps because the joy of acquisition is tinged with reverence.

Look at the growing number of Japanese conductors, instrumentalists, singers. They have become incontrovertible experts in Western arts. The bow in our direction is not a mere formality. It is also the result of a rich discovery.

2 November 1990

Eternal Rumours

Twice in a short while I have fallen foul of summit meetings, entering, as it were, by the tradesmen's entrance. There I have suffered the inevitable buffeting from those in charge of the elaborate security arrangements which are the pride of every host country. It is interesting to see how these differ. New York is a relatively recent city, laid out according to a plan. Consequently, it was possible during the Children's summit a few weeks ago to isolate certain prescribed avenues which had the doubtful advantage that the fearful congestion elsewhere in the city could be described as virtually normal. The major difficulty was for those with passes to penetrate into areas blocked by passless spectators, eager to catch glimpses of famous faces even through the inky windows of stretch limousines.

Every effort to push forward to a checkpoint was regarded with hostility as though I were cheating on the rules of precedence which are acknowledged the world over, right down to the bread queues in Moscow. I was saved by a huge fellow wearing a blue bullet-proof vest with the words 'US Secret Service' embossed on it in fluorescent letters.

The problems of security in Rome are somewhat different. The city developed illogically over seven hills and is dubbed eternal by virtue of its ability to survive in a hostile world. Its frequent occupations by foreign powers mean that, by now, rumour is a far more potent instrument than mere information. Crowds do not gather to stare. They either participate or they stay away, grumble at impossible traffic conditions and spread rumours.

Last week I was in Rome to promote a book of mine and I was not surprised to find the foyer of the hotel, selected for me by the publishers, invaded by a trio of Alsatian dogs controlled by rather puny handlers who had considerable difficulty keeping their charges under control, excited as these were by the ceaseless coming and going of customers and their rich perfumes.

It was then that I learned that a European summit was in progress and rumour had it that several leaders of the continent were staying there. One employee said he had picked out both Bush and Andreotti on their way to their rooms. I managed to scotch both rumours, at least locally, by pointing out that Bush was not European and that Andreotti would hardly be staying in an hotel where he had a home.

Later in the day, after many interviews, I wanted an espresso. I called room service. When nothing happened after half an hour, I opened the door to find myself face to face with another Alsatian dog whose eyes shone in the dark like the barrels of two guns. I understood why my call for room service had not been answered.

I had kept one day free for shopping and mere ambling. My wife and I booked at a restaurant for 1pm, only to find that taxis vere virtually non-existent since a huge union rally had added to the confusion imposed by the summit. Once again, rumours were the only things that found no travel restrictions. Since Italy is also the land of miracles, a non-existent taxi pulled up and we were able to go to the restaurant through practically empty streets. We were told, before leaving the hotel, that we would have to leave as early as 5pm to catch a plane at 8.35. Three and a half hours? Why? Rumour had it, they explained. We ordered a car for five.

Leaving the restaurant just before three, we were met

by a rain storm which is fatal for window-shopping since you go in to avoid the rain. Now there really were no taxis and no miracles either. Our hotel, being on one of the capital's steepest hills, only saw us shortly before five as we panted our way up the final incline.

'When's your plane?' asked the driver.

'8.35.'

He pulled a wry face. 'Hope we've left enough time,' he said. 'Damned summit. They're just ego-trips. Get nothing done.'

Despite rumours, there were no obstructions whatever. We arrived at the airport at 5.25. The airline offices were shut until 7.30. We sat on a trolley and took it in turns to doze off, the one awake to keep an eye on the luggage.

A few days later, Sir Geoffrey Howe resigned. Even if the summits are just ego-trips, they do get things done after all. Rumour has it . . .

9 November 1990

Divided Loyalties

I maintain that those of us in liberal professions really have two loyalties – that of our passport and that of our discipline. At a time in which interest in the human condition is growing at the expense of the increasingly lacklustre game of politics, it is not unusual to re-examine the meaning of words as they are bandied about like weightless shuttlecocks. What is a conservative, for instance?

A young fellow who gives the impression he was born to rule and therefore smilingly maintains that every electoral setback is merely temporary? In the Soviet Union, a conservative could mean a supporter of the late Mr Brezhnev and a centralized economy. In Japan, it could refer to those who believe in the divinity of the royal house and the rosy future of belligerency.

The sobriquet could even be attached to the statement of a revered backbencher of the British party of that name, who said he was sick and tired of hearing the relatives of Gulf hostages mewling and puking (poor Shakespeare) on the box. Sorrow, he suggested, is a private affair and the traditional stiff upper lip should be brought into play. But conservatism isn't all tastelessness and obduracy, pride and patriotism.

What word could better describe those who brave the elements to drive or be driven in vehicles constructed before the year 1904 from London to Brighton in November? First of all, is it not astonishing that 478 entries should have been received from owners with cars in working order, constructed between 1884 and 1904?

Working order is, of course, a bit of an exaggeration

since only just over 400 made it to the starting grid but, all the same, it does seem a staggering quantity of the best kind of conservative, those with loyalties to a discipline. The discipline in question concerns respect, the kind of living respect that would be accorded Isosceles for his triangle or Harvey for his bloodstream, not a vaguely comic retro-genuflection in the direction of archaic practices.

There are those utterly unsentimental spirits, and the great French aircraft and motorcar designer Gabriel Voisin was among them, who believe in progress to the point of never even glimpsing the rear-view mirror. To largely American fanatics eager to seek advice on rebuilding his cars, he used to snap: 'Buy a Citroen 2CV. It's better than anything we were able to build at the time.'

But there are those others for whom the achievements of the past are as precious, and as worthy of nursing, as the rarest of plants, the most august of trees. In short, there are those who regard the ancient horseless carriage as an endangered species.

Europe, the Europe of loyalty to this ideal, was the cradle of the motor vehicle at a time when no threat to the environment could possibly have been envisaged. Nor could the early cars be considered as an expression of machismo. In fact, the earliest entry in the rally, a French De Dion Bouton, was demurely described as a Dos-a-Dos, or Back-to-Back. By 1893, this had already been amended by the mighty Benz factory, with a Vis-à-Vis, or Face-to-Face. The rot set in about a century ago.

The Europe in question is not the fortress so feared by those outside it, but the open, free and quietly majestic Europe to which those of sensibility owe allegiance.

To be driven by Prince Michael of Kent in a 1904 Mercedes Simplex was a lesson in democracy and in solidarity. The enthusiasm of the crowds who lined the route meant that the role of navigator was supplanted by that of waver. To those unfortunate people stranded by the wayside, either lying under their horseless carriages or sitting disconsolately on the running-boards, every kind of help was forthcoming.

And lest it be thought that this was merely an outing for individual fanatics, the car I was in was an exhibit in the Mercedes Benz Museum; others emanated from Jaguar Daimler, Ford, Vauxhall and Rover as well as Lord Montagu's National Motor Museum and the Science Museum.

The powerful industrial corporations are the first to realise the importance of firm and loving links with their origins. It is possible – even desirable – to be progressive and conservative.

16 November 1990

Shielding a Real Threat

Imminent Thunder indeed! Who on earth invents these coarse names for threatening gestures which are supposed to be subtle signals to a potential enemy? As though 'Desert Shield' were not clumsy enough as a declaration of intention, we must now get used to a new phrase – the name given to landing exercises on the Saudi coast – as the sand-caked shield is laboriously hammered into an offensive weapon.

Is there a committee of superannuated military chiefs, judiciously mingled with a few respected civilian and religious authorities, who are charged with thinking up these aberrations? One speculates with alarm on the ideas which must have been rejected on the way to the solution. 'Greased Lightning' for instance. That was surely rejected as giving away the potential speed of the onslaught. It could have dropped a hint to the Iraqis and destroyed all elements of surprise.

'Desert Spear' someone suggested. The consensus was that this might look like a shift in policy and that is certainly not the case. The posture might be seen as being a defensive one, even if it becomes necessary to defend oneself all the way to Baghdad and beyond.

'Wrath of the Prophet' was another idea. It was feared that, although this had the virtue of wresting the spiritual initiative from Saddam Hussein's hypocritical grasp, it might be construed as interference in Saudi prerogatives, and therefore disruptive.

It was probably way beyond lunchtime, that moment at which other considerations begin to impinge on the purity of concentration, that someone said: 'How about Imminent Thunder?' After the briefest of reflections, they agreed it was great. Their febrile fingers fumbled with the locks of their briefcases and they hurried off to previous engagements, brimful of apologies for being late.

Of course, all this is guesswork, but the kind of guesswork born of long experience. There used to be an instruction on the bedpans in night trains clattering up to Scotland many years ago which said, in words which gave every indication of having been carefully chosen: 'Passengers are reminded that these receptacles were not designed to receive solids.' Can you imagine the committee meeting which arrived at this sterling example of administrative taste mingled with relentless objectivity? What would really have been entertaining were the endless discussions leading up to this result.

In Rome, a city of splendid monuments, there is that famous monstrosity called 'The Altar of the Nation' by the few tasteless Italians in existence. It is that gigantic marble pile which throws its encumbered shadow over Piazza Venezia, an orgy of fin-de siècle filigree.

Some clever publisher brought out a book of the rejected designs submitted for this same monument. One is led to the reluctant and amazed conclusion that, even if the actual monument is a bit like the Albert Memorial with elephantiasis, it is still considerably better than its competitors and thoroughly deserved to win the competition. Once again, the discussions leading up to its selection would have been eminently worth hearing.

I caught one of the wittiest men of my youth, the film producer John Sutro, gazing in admiration at an Edwardian hat rack in a provincial hotel. Pre-Raphaelite nymphs cavorted in abundance on the dark oak panel out of which the rack grew like the horns of a stag at bay. 'I like to think of that being chosen,' he said. I knew what he meant. The ephemeral pros and cons which led to such an acquisition. The diverting clash between bad taste and worse taste. Well,

RUDOLF VALENTINO

AND

NORMA SCHWARZKOPF

IN

DESERT STORM

the pros and cons are still at loggerheads.

'Imminent Thunder' is the latest fruit of their cogitations. It expresses eloquently the puerile quality of a resolve eroded by doubts and anxieties in the hearts and minds of ordinary people. These can only grow with the passage of time. Give sanctions and ostracism a chance and may the thunder remain, for ever imminent.

23 November 1990

A Winning Way to Lose

So, the unthinkable has occurred. An event which both supporters and detractors believed impossible. The lady, it turns out, was neither for burning nor for turning, merely perhaps for yearning, if and when she is kicked upstairs to the House of Lords. It is not my wish to dwell for too long on a situation which has perhaps exhausted its capacity for surprising, and caused a multitude of typhoons in a great many teacups. Suffice it to say that for all its international repercussions – perhaps because of them – it remains a peculiarly British event.

The lady herself was acclaimed, by many of those eager to be rid of her, as the greatest of peacetime prime ministers. The distinction was made retrospectively, with a tactfully suppressed sign of relief, in order not to affect Churchill's position in the history books. It is a curious one for the lady, so personable, kind and considerate in private, was far better known as her alter-ego, the warrior queen of surpassing arrogance and almost risible overstatement.

The peculiar values of the British way are characterised by the legend above the 'gladiators' entrance' at Wimbledon, a quote from Kipling's poem, 'If' which prepared the players for both the dangers of victory and the opportunities of defeat. Let me explain this apparent paradox.

In British public schools students are taught to lose with such elegance that the winner is denied the full taste of victory. This may, of course, have led to the habit of losing which has, at times, become a blight of almost plague-like proportions among British sporting teams. Never mind, it is already a triumph if they are masters of at least one great art, that of losing to one's advantage.

The lady certainly has a temperament which rises to occasions. Without an occasion to rise to, she can be mournful, monotonous, even dull. But once there's an occasion, look out – even it it is one which promises something less than elation.

She rose to such an occasion and, in the best tradition of Kipling and the Wimbledon Centre Court, turned it to her advantage. 'I'm enjoying this,' she cried as she transformed a valedictory moment into a festival of high good humour. The effect on the victorious was immediate. Sworn enemies vied in finding embarrassing superlatives in the hope of stealing fragments of thunder that were irrevocably lost, so blinding was the lightning.

Whatever induced the opposition Labour Party to launch a motion of no-confidence into this internecine battle, nobody will ever know. Surely that was a moment for a low profile, enabling the conspirators in the Conservative Party to stew in their own juices. Even those who had merely expressed opinions sub-rosa suddenly appeared as assassins or, even worse, as traitors. The motion, which was predestined to be defeated, gave the disrupted Conservative ranks the illusion of cohesion. And this, thanks to Labour.

And that is not all. The whole amazing incident, including the lady's sacrifice, has turned into a gigantic public-relations operation. Asked which of the three candidates people in the street would select, the reply always seemed to imply that a new prime minister was being chosen for a full parliamentary term, not merely a new leader for the Conservatives, capable of losing an election.

During all this, we all neglected to think of the Labour leader Mr Kinnock. The self-defeating attempt to overthrow a government which was down but not

94

MRS. THATCHER HEARING
HER VOICE

out, hardly made us remember him other than as a buoyant and charming fellow with a suspect sense of occasion. The one thing in his favour was that Foreign Secretary Mr Hurd, upright to the point of stiffness, deigned to refer to him as a lightweight. Accustomed as we now are to the boring, and painfully predictable slanging match between the parties, this disparaging slight served to remind us that the office makes the man, and indeed the woman, and that Mr Kinnock and Liberal Democrat leader Mr Ashdown are no doubt capable of rising to all sorts of unexpected occasions.

Meanwhile, we watched the three candidates hawk their wares, Mr Hurd attempted a more popular style. 'It just ain't so,' he said the other day, quickly correcting himself to 'it just isn't so', in case his attempt at jocularity be thought of as a lapse. Mr Major is evidently trying to appear older than he is and Mr Heseltine works at being measured and reliable in order to counteract the wayward romanticism of his hair. At all events, the whole catalogue of surprises remind us that Shakespeare was a true English genius and that Julius Caesar is nothing to do with ancient Rome, but rather with contemporary Britain. Et tu, Heseltine? Et tu, Major? Et tu, Hurd? At least times have changed, if little else. The plotters all had rubber daggers.

30 November 1990

Of Bards and Braces

At the moment at which men meet for the first time face to face under the Channel, it is perhaps in order to let a few tiny kittens out of their bags. The English and the French have been busy misunderstanding each other for as long as there has been anything to misunderstand. 'Fair stood the wind for France,' the poet wrote. Far from being a happy augury from the Meteorological Office to a travel agent, this merely meant that the lads should ready their arrows because the landing would occur sooner than anyone had dared hope. On a similar occasion, someone in the know must have used a variation of this phrase to William the Conqueror but, of course, in French.

You only have to look at the caricatures of the past to understand the full measure of incomprehension and the unrestrained passion with which this pastime of misunderstanding was pursued. At the time of the Napoleonic Wars, the English inevitably appeared as joyously belching carnivorous gentlemen whose knees disappear in folds of fat raddled with gout and who seem to epitomize a certain concept of health in an aura of unrestrained surrender to pleasure. The French are depicted as foreign to the gastronomic arts, wizened, aquiline creatures, victims of their own futile ambitions and chaotic inability to organise any antidote to their own chronic undernourishment. They are poor and thin, while the English are bulbous and wealthy.

Even their senses of occasion are different. Take war memorials, for instance. The English ones are stiffly understated with mourning Tommies standing to attention, their helmets dipping over their eyes to hide all forms of expression. On the French ones, the Poilu is usually lying in a sea of mud next to a shattered artillery wheel, his arm outstretched towards a massive angel which casts its gloomy shadow over the scene of heroic destruction. The soldier has invariably lost his helmet in the fray while his English counterpart is never, even in the hell of the trenches, improperly dressed.

Perhaps I may take you into the wings of solemnity on both sides of the Channel. As a foreigner to both traditions I have been allowed to savour their charm and peculiarities. This privilege came to me quite by surprise on both occasions. My mind goes back to that splendid room in Buckingham Palace used for rehearsals before investitures. A group of elderly gentlemen, two of them in kilts, stood around shyly like new boys in some august seat of learning. Before them was a well-worn footstool with a raised railing. At first glance it looked disconcertingly like a rather fragile block on which the head was supposed to rest before a beheading, but an officer in formal attire put an end to our anxiety.

'Step smartly forward,' he said, 'once you have advanced a couple of paces into the room and turn as smartly to the left. Three paces should see you to the edge of the footstool. Two for the inordinately tall, four for the exceptionally small, but I see no one here answering to those descriptions, so three should do it. Once in the immediate proximity of the footstool, you should be facing Her Majesty. Now lean forward to grasp the railing with your right hand, at the same time extending your left leg forward and sideways at an angle of 45 degrees, and beginning to flex the right knee. It's quite simple really. If you panic, watch the man in front of you and do likewise. That is, if you are convinced that he is doing the right thing. If not, for goodness' sake try to remember what I have told you.'

He ended by scolding us as though we had already

got into a hopeless muddle. We were allowed several dry runs at the footstool, like apprentice pilots attempting to land on an aircraft carrier, far below us in a sea of Turkish carpet. All went well, thank Heaven, although it was a little surprising to experience this moment of consecration to the tones of *South Pacific* played by a suitably restrained military band.

The difference between this and the entrance to the French Academy is that there every new boy is on his own in a jungle of prefects. There is no intake, only individuals to replace the late lamented. But the changing room is common to them all, a room with many doors like a Feydeau farce. On great occasions it overflows with noble academicians in thermal underwear, variously complaining: 'I'll have to go without my sword, my wife mislaid the belt.' 'Do what I do, carry it.' 'D'you think they'll notice I've got red socks' 'Not if you let your pants down – loosen the braces, man, loosen the braces. Don't look so damned helpless!'

Finally, a common humanity lies at the base of all traditions and a smile is never far below any glittering surface.

7 December 1990

A Whisper from God

It was not for a moment the threat of military confrontation which brought about changes in Eastern Europe, however much those favouring obsolete assessments of such things may like to congratulate themselves. For some time now, armed strength has not been able to achieve much, outside places like Chad that is, and then on a very limited scale. Vietnam is generally regarded as a mistaken initiative and certainly the power available just could not be used. The same is true of Afghanistan.

Even as far back as 1914 the rot was already beginning to set in. The experts talked of 'a war over by Christmas'. Christmas 1914, that is. In 1939, the Germans launched what they called a Blitzkrieg. It started well enough for them, this lightning war, but finally became entangled in the undergrowth and dragged on endlessly, with enormous loss of life and human dignity.

Now this ageing monster is being summoned from its slumbers yet again, with talk of a sudden, swift and surgical operation in the Gulf. That indispensable element of surprise, no doubt, which, before long, turns to surprise that the whole exercise should still be going on so long after the first rapid strike. That calculated first round k.o. too often ends as a split decision.

What has caused this degradation of sabre-rattling to an also-ran among the shower of news items which claim our attention at every moment?

It is surely the media which has taken over as a battleground for the conflicts of nations, from the less eloquent, less entertaining, less intelligent cannons. The Eastern Europeans changed direction overnight because their ideological armour, which was thought to be impregnable, turned out to be porous. News of the Outer World seeped through until the fabric of State was saturated and the entire structure began to collapse.

That, and not the other man's missiles, brought about the extraordinary changes in our world. The weapons of tomorrow's wars are television, telephone, telefax, right up to spy satellites and future means of communication.

We all know almost everything about each other. The Americans study Iraq with all their extraordinary armoury of sophisticated equipment. Saddam Hussein, less well served, contents himself by watching Cable News Network. Who can say which is better off?

What is evident, however, is that Saddam Hussein, with his subtle changes of position, has so far made an infinitely better use of the media than the masters of the art, Bush and Baker, whose inflexibility is bad public relations by any standards, even if it is A1 integrity.

Saddam Hussein has quite recently discovered God and perhaps the satellites caught the moment of re-birth without immediately interpreting this miracle as a shrewd overture to the Arab world. His odyssey, after the initial gaffe of seizing Kuwait in the time-honoured way of military dictators, is a fascinating one, as he rolls with every predictable punch from the opposition.

Hostages became guests to be released in dribs and drabs as eminent visitors queued up to talk him out of his intractability.

Then, suddenly convinced that these guests were a liability rather than an asset, he released them all in a magnanimous gesture of seasonal goodwill, even pausing to apologize for his error of judgment and asking God's forgiveness for any inconvenience caused.

And this fellow, soft spoken to the point of inaudibility, is the latter-day Hitler we must not appease at any cost. His initial faux pas is obvious, but the absurdity of such a comparison makes the wisdom of those who propagate it suspect, to say the least.

Of course, the enormous reticence of even the most rabid hawks, faced with an inevitability of armed conflict, is very clear and even quite moving. Once again, this is due to the generally high standard of information and the fact that, if the horrors of war are unleashed, they will erupt in the drawing-rooms of the world as well as on the battlefield itself. The television coverage will be as unrelentingly thorough as the weapons themselves and their results could be as unpredictable, as alarming.

Never has public opinion been as volatile as it is today; thanks to television, any slight shift of emphasis, any miscalculation of the popular mood could, in a trice, change the general perception of the events as they occur, and the public has a way of making its views known. Many recent leaders from both East and West have reason to acknowledge this phenomenon as well as the speed with which previously accepted moral ascendancy is challenged.

The mood in general is not one for warfare. With the destructive power of modern weapons in mind, the reasons for going to war would have to be overwhelming to be convincing. They are not. And Mr Bush's remark that the departure of the hostages from Iraq renders it easier to countenance military action will hardly make them so. What it needs now is for God, in his infinite understanding, to whisper to Saddam Hussein that there are certain advantages in not hanging on to Kuwait. Then we can pretend again that the threat of war has done the trick.

14 December 1990

Prejudice Flourishes

There are those, some of them in important positions, who still see the world through the perspective of their youth, a time which evidently has had such an impact on the men and women they have become that no change of thinking is still possible. The fact that among those ossified are people of great mental and spiritual quality makes it no easier to bear as a phenomenon. On the contrary.

Let me give an example. There is a very real fear among even thoughtful elements in many countries that Europe will eradicate all national character, that this cherished continent will undergo a kind of levelling worse than death.

What was the reality when the majority of those who share these fears were young? It was a Europe in which only the rich travelled and they went only where other rich congregated. The most ignoble, the most degrading prejudices were rampant, caused amusement and were even deemed to be true. Armies were still instruments of potential conquest, not yet harbingers of total annihilation. Europe was not only divided hopelessly against itself but the festering of its wounds caused the two greatest conflagrations in the history of mankind. Are we really justified in indulging in nostalgia for all that? Was any part of it worth preserving? Was it an example for the Third World to follow, that heritage of insolvent chaos left over from the days of colonial arrogance? National character will never, can never, be eradicated. Without it there can be no Europe, it is the charm of Europe. Why then should there be fear that that which cannot disappear, will disappear?

Those who live in the shadow of this impossible threat have seen their intellects and capabilities develop at the expense of their eyes and ears. Somehow they deal with the most complicated abstractions in utter serenity, without really noticing what goes on around them or listening to the nuances of the voices they hear.

Some while ago I ran into a distinguished London solicitor in the Champs-Elysées in Paris. He had obviously braved the Channel to discuss some complicated legal entanglements with a French counterpart. On that level he was certainly a great expert and would speak with enviable lucidity. In order to place his French interlocutors at ease, he wore traditional black with striped trousers. On his head, a beret.

I asked him, as tactfully as possible, what on earth he thought he was doing. He answered me tersely, even tetchily, that in his view, when in Rome . . . I told him it was a charming thought but could he see another beret in the Champs-Elysées? He was sure he could. What a stupid and unobservant remark of mine. After a minute he panicked. Where had they all gone?

Here was a case in point. As his mind developed logically to encompass all the complicated issues of contemporary litigation, he was literally working in the dark. His windows on the world had been firmly shut since his youth and the curtains drawn. Despite the teeming evidence of the street, to him the average Frenchman wore a beret and smelled of garlic.

A famous politician, who has had sufficient exposure recently for me to impose the censorship of anonymity, told me before the upheavals in Eastern Europe that there was no public opinion in the Soviet Union. That someone well versed in a certain view of politics should make such an assertion came as no surprise, but for it to be made by one who also had pretensions to know human nature (as part of the job of administration) was frankly alarming. Where there are people there is always public opinion, and prejudice also – that sediment of education which lies buried at the base of human consciousness.

Those who fear German reunion still think in terms of massed infantry sweeping across the peaceful landscapes of Flanders and the Ukraine, as though land could still be conquered in this day and age. It can merely be devastated, of no further use to victor or vanquished. Under such circumstances, Germany, with her enormous industrial potential and capacity for concentration on the matters in hand, is an invaluable asset in the structure of the modern, open Europe. After so many centuries of misbehaviour, due to what is cynically and quite erroneously called 'Enlightened National Interest', it is high time that we allow ourselves to conceive of a world in which traditional enmity plays no further part. It is quite possible, and now is certainly the moment. The only discordant note is a realisation that both Churchill and De Gaulle were far more modern and clairvoyant than their successors. Right up to the end their windows were never shut, their curtains never drawn.

21 December 1990

Sign of the Season

We find ourselves in the period of the great paradox: goodwill towards all men and considerable irritation to boot. Huge Father Christmases nod at us from many shop windows in this age of the robot, accompanied by coyly humanized reindeer, while people slip and shudder in the cold outside. To dream of a White Christmas is to be pretty clairvoyant about cancelled means of transport, traffic jams, the threat of broken limbs and other products of natural inclemency.

I spent last week in commercial activity like most other people. Christmas is not conducive to creativity of any kind. It is a season in which heartiness tends to preempt affection, good cheer replaces well being and songs are sung in unison, not parts.

For all these reasons I spent my time signing books of mine in bookshops throughout Germany. That is about as low a profile as I could manage. It entailed clearing the mind of all temptations to communicate on an ambitious scale. Even conversation was impossible with the people as they lined up to have their book inscribed, since it would have been unfair to those waiting in line.

Still, there were some curious encounters. A lad came in with a shaved head, apart from a spine of stunted hair which traversed his iron-grey skull from widow's peak to leather collar. His ears were a mass of brass studs with several punched cruelly into the sides of his nostrils.

'What do you want me to write?' I asked.

'Just your name,' he replied, with surprising lucidity. 'No date. I bring you much respect from the skinheads of Kreuzberg.'

It was like a vote of confidence, as well as a kind of declaration of independence from stereotyped rituals. Most German readers insist on the date. They are great ones for anniversaries, for recollection, for ordered memory. Some have very specific requests. 'To my mother, on her 80th' and the like.

They show anything from surprise to deep resentment when I point out that I am unable to dedicate it to 'My mother.'

'Why not?' they tend to inquire, 'Is there something you don't like about my mother?'

'Nothing, except that she's your mother, not mine. If I dedicate the book to your mother, I can't write "My mother".'

Cups of coffee are brought, and honey cakes nestle among pine cones and silver streamers. There could be no forgetting the imminence of Christmas. Of the great majority who want dates, some demand a specific birthday, others are divided between the 24th and 25th and even ask for both with a hyphen in between.

In between these signing sessions, there were palpable examples of the Christmas spirit in action: the launching of the first of many aircraft by the Johanniter, the German wing of the St John's Ambulance Brigade; these took off for Minsk loaded with food and medicine.

As I tottered across Cologne airport with a sackful of flour for loading, I was asked if I would accompany this ecumenical mission, involving Lutheran and Catholic charities in help destined for the Orthodox Metropolitan of Minsk. I replied that my weight in powdered milk would be more appreciated at this time.

A further charity in a circus tent, with clowns as waiters, and the launching of the Unicef State of the World's Children Report with James Grant, the Secretary General of the organization, and Richard von Weizsäcker, the President of the now united Germany, as chief orators, showed to what extent the new Germany accepts its responsibilities as a free and powerful nation within Europe.

It is natural that the Germans, after their particular historical experience, feel very drawn towards ecology and other simple eternal values. Gorbachev is even more popular here than anywhere else in Europe. They realize who has most helped them towards unity, and they give thanks with impressive and laudable generosity.

What with one thing and another, all these seasonal quirks have really given Father Christmas and his reindeer reasons to nod, even after the shops shut.

28 December 1990

Flight from Festivity

I must confess to an almost Scrooge-like distaste for Christmas. The endless electronic carillon, the feverish commercial activity, the routine calls from newspapers or television programmes hawking around for some original thoughts on the theme, all these make me wish to flee the developed world. We did just that, my wife and I. With seasonal snow visible as far as the eye could see we packed our scantiest clothes and set out far beyond the horizon and the gung-ho-ho.

The flight to Bangkok was uneventful except for an occasional turbulence which set the clusters of white and silver Christmas decorations above our heads juddering. The decorations were excusable since we were travelling on a European airline. Soon it would all be different.

The caressing sounds of plaintive Oriental voices belonged to those who worshipped other gods and celebrated other anniversaries, those for whom goodwill was part of their creed, who needed no reminding at a specific moment of the year.

The first impact of real heat was like the lifting of a veil. We sank into a voluptuous torpor, negligent of time and the lost hours, basking in the half-light of siesta until further notice. It came, brutally, that further notice, under our window, like a ghostly serenade conjured up by Dickens himself, in sentimental, roistering mood.

It was a bell, rung with the insistence of a boarding house lunch gong, accompanied by peals of forced laughter. One glance through the mosquito netting was enough to establish the presence of Father Christmas under our window, accompanied by dwarfs, in an orgy of red and cotton wool.

The noise continued. Soon it became evident that solitude and the world of dreams were over. If you can't beat them, join them, as the saying goes. Dressing quickly, we joined the tumult.

Father Christmas was most cordial, ringing his bell as though his life depended on it and blowing raspberries on an aged motor horn. From the depths, behind the paroxysm of cotton wool, came a gruff but friendly American voice: 'How ya doin'?' The dwarfs were Thai children having the time of their lives in an alien tradition.

The outdoor buffet was sumptuous, as befits a hotel held by many to be the most extraordinary in the world. We sat under the stars beside the Chao Phraya river and listened to a choir of Thai schoolgirls singing carols. They were dressed as though attending a distinguished British public school and they sang in flawless English, French, German and Latin.

They were followed by discreet rock and roll, if there is such a thing, for dancing. At the next table a large family of Danes churned out carols of their own in dogged counterpoint to the more modern thumping of the orchestra.

Gradually our churlish opposition to the celebration dissolved in the warmth of the evening, an emotional as well as physical temperature. And its spirit seems to be enduring.

On the morning of the 26th one of the superbly trained staff bowed in my direction, his nose held in the narrow pyramid of his arched hands, and muttered 'Milly Kissmiss'. Since then, others have done the same, noticeably the pair of cleaning ladies who dropped their vacuum-cleaner tube as I opened the door to them, cupped their hands over their noses and said in chorus: 'Milly Kissmiss'.

If no stop is put to this, I could foresee this phrase continuing deep into the summer. By then, ethnically inquisitive tourists will no doubt take this for some traditional Thai greeting, cup their hands over their noses in deference to local custom, and repeat 'Milly Kissmiss' in the belief that they have taken the first step in penetrating the mysteries of Oriental courtesy.

Elsewhere in the world, in the sands of Saudi Arabia, the same message of goodwill prevails, but with a proviso that it must be temporarily suspended at midnight on 14 January. One's heart goes out to those new hostages of the desert and the cruel limits to their spirit of Christmas.

To them, and to all my readers, I bow deferentially, cup my nose in my hands and say, 'Milly Kissmiss'. This message from the prehistoric mists of Thai folklore will long outlive all examples of man's intolerance to man.

4 January 1991

Disarming Warriors

Apart from the deplorable hiccough of the Gulf, the general tendency has been towards disarmament. Even experts have begun to concede that the concept of conquest has been replaced by that of total destruction. This poses the problem of what we can do with all those gloomy battleships in mothballs which look like great-grandfather elephants moving miserably to their final resting place.

What do we do with the missile casings, the rusty Kalashnikovs, the kilometres of camouflage netting and old boots? I have an idea. The urge towards military glory is evidently so deeply ingrained in human nature that there are still those who spend their weekends attacking each other, more vocally than physically, in reserved sections of public parkland, wearing grotesque masks, shrieking and firing harmless bullets at each other.

Quite clearly, here is a lack which will be sorely felt once the consensus of civilised humanity decides that such activities tend towards the abnormal. Where will the secretly bellicose go to indulge their vice? Will they become as silent and ingrowing as were the gays in the past, or as horrifyingly clandestine as the paedophiles seem to be now? One hopes not. The world cannot afford any more underground movements, any more terrorists of the unquiet spirit.

Surely the answer lies in theme parks, those ingenious places where fantasies can be indulged without danger to law-abiding citizens. Today it is certainly possible to wander innocently into the middle of an improvised conflict between two self-imposed battle groups, to be superficially wounded by a distinguished stockbroker on his day off, or to suffer a heart attack as a frustrated scoutmaster leaps at you out of a bush. In the theme parks, as I conceive them, these imponderables of the quiet country ramble would be things of the past.

Already our civilization abounds in computerized games in which the arts of war and the techniques of sport are demystified. Now the theme parks would carry the dreams a step closer to the reality which is the goal of every lethal reverie. It would be possible in these outdoor temples of counterfeit destruction to relive some of the great battles of history and come up with different results from those in the history books.

Agincourt and Crècy could be reconceived and the French could well turn out to be the winners, at least in theme parks near Paris. At the new theme park near Spandau, in which stones from the Wall could be used liberally as evidence of debris, there could well be the reconstruction of the Allied surrender of 1918, with the role of the Kaiser brilliantly enacted by some old codger harbouring a smouldering resentment against the injustice of Versailles.

But these are only ideas for those so far gone down the road of illusion that they believe the whole of history is only there for reassessment. And such diversions hardly help us with the problem of the profitable utility of more recent military material. The manufacture of arrows with suction caps for medieval conflict is a problem all its own.

Certainly, modern conflict will be the main lure of the parks. There will be sections not only for participation but for spectator sports. Is it too much to hope for a wooded part of the landscape in which some general officers, fallen on unforeseeable hard times by virtue of premature retirement, eke out little supplements to their pensions by crawling about with binoculars at the ready and giving instructions into field telephones?

The whole is rendered more thrilling and more unpredictable by the insidious presence of miscalculation and chaos (as in real battle) which entails the sudden appearance of an enemy patrol and the generals' surrender.

The public will be asked not to feed the officers between truces so that these do not become spoiled by a too frequent realization of what they once were.

Children would, of course, be admitted to these places. Their enthusiasm for this kind of pastime is, on the whole, as intense as that of many adults, but it has a shorter wind. They would have to be told they had been the principal victims of the real thing in the past. They could fire the guns of huge, derelict tanks at cut-out dummies, fire machine-guns at toy aircraft, sink with the *Bismarck* or the *Hood* in a tank of temperate water a few inches deep, into which the superstructure of old ships had been lowered.

There would be any amount of ways in which the young in years and the young in heart could get the rubbish out of their systems. And perhaps, towards tea time, after the rigours of war had been tasted as a tray full of canapés, parents and youngsters might repair for a square meal to the Saddam restaurant where there is no menu, no food and no drink, because here at least sanctions have been allowed to work.

After dark, a few mutilated tapes of Bob Hope can be bought at exorbitant prices from shady street vendors who hover round the gates of every theme park, selling medals and other less salubrious things.

You wanted war, didn't you?

11 January 1991

114

Satellites of Truth

One remembers the upheavals at Unesco several years ago which inspired the United States, and subsequently the United Kingdom, to slam the doors on the organization until further notice: a notice which has not yet been given. The basis of the disagreement was ostensibly the authoritarian manner of the then secretary-general, but this issue was complicated by the fact that the incumbent was the only African to occupy a post of such influence within the United Nations family and seemed to have become a champion of the aspirations of Third World countries at the expense of the interests of some established opinion leaders.

The major bone of contention was the setting up of independent news agencies in countries small and new to furnish local needs. This was taken by some major powers to be an effort to control the news nefariously and to influence what is affectionately and erroneously called 'the truth'.

While admitting that Unesco has changed immeasurably and for the better since those days, I have always felt that there was a basic flaw in the Western stance. News is, by its very nature, tendentious. Its source always has to be taken into consideration, as well as the particular eyes or ears to which it is diffused. The important news agencies may all report the truth, but it is *their* truth and, without even a hint of it being editorialised, it inevitably bears the colour of its origin. A chandelier in a room can be seen by all but everyone in that room sees it from his own angle. So it is with the truth or, rather, 'the truth'.

At the moment in Thailand I find myself admirably

placed to remember these circumstances and make these comments. It is not that we are out of touch in this segment of paradise where everything conspires to make us forget the weight of the world's problems; it is that we are separated from the news by a larger lapse of time than is usual these days. Admittedly, there are the English-language newspapers, both of them surprisingly good and with excellent comments on events, but they arrive fairly late in the day. Then there is the television and here we run into difficulties hardly foreseeable in the original row in Unesco.

Thailand has a censorship which is both rigorous and benevolent. There is no point to censorship unless it is rigorous, and the benevolence seems to fit the smiling and meditative character of the people. That character appears to be true until you catch a Thai boxing match on another channel, when there are suddenly no smiles and little meditation.

As for the censorship, nobody can explain its purpose even if its reasons can be put down to the inordinate quantity of generals in the government or hovering in its vicinity. Suffice it to say, the results are only perceptible to an outsider in the programmes of that admirable organisation, CNN, which are not projected live. The consequence of this need for official review is a certain degree of chaos. In one report Saddam has agreed to talks, in the next he has refused, simply because the earlier report was placed later to give the later report precedence. The height of confusion was reached when the most recent analysis of the situation in the Gulf was announced to give way to a brief but animated conversation between Mrs Thatcher and Mr Shevardnadze, which made one realize, if nothing else, that time really does fly.

CNN and Sky News are two of the reasons why the bars of the prisons in eastern Europe snapped. They have pre-empted news agencies as diffusers of 'the truth'. Although CNN boasts it brings events to the viewer without editorial comment, this is neither their final aim nor their achievement. A CNN journalist praised the new image of the UN, declaring that soon its secretary-general would be more a general than a secretary, and that the US seems to be calling the shots. Pat Buchanan, CNN's rampant patriot, regards the world as just another American problem, along with the economy and abortion. Norman Tebbit, cast in a similar role for Sky News, emphasizes the difference in temperament between two peoples who are on the same side in most things and, yet, complementary rather than alike. He applies common-sense where it has no place.

But let us finish in Thailand. All I have ever caught on their news is the election of Miss Thailand, which seemed to spread over several days, and in which they were all too considerate of the feelings of the losers to announce a winner. One striking aspect of this was that none of the competitors were small, slight or exquisite. They were all very much alike: huge, leggy and with identical bouffant coiffures. Thailand is, evidently, determined to be competitive in the modern world.

10 January 1991

Airing the Vital Issues

It is impossible to be light-hearted at this time, which marks an enormous and salutary change in the habits of this planet. Somebody's grandfather said that if the battles on the Somme in the First World War had been recorded on television that would have ended warfare once and for all. There is no reason to doubt this. In fact, as a result of sheer revulsion at the sinful waste and stupidity of battle the instincts of a large section of humanity already gravitate towards peaceful solutions to problems.

The innocent victims of war – men, women and children – care not at all about the origin of the weapons that kill or maim them. Death is death, whether it comes in the form of a missile launched by a madman or from a source convinced of its moral ascendancy. Only the survivors see a difference and allow their prejudices to colour the hypocrisy without which all conflict quickly loses its meaning.

There are many disconcerting aspects to this unique moment in the story of mankind when the weapons of war have been pulled out of their hiding-places like the paraphernalia of long-forgotten carnivals – one hopes for the last time. Among them are the untroubled expression on Saddam Hussein's face and the terrible loneliness of President Bush whose arched eyebrows are symptomatic of doubt and, therefore, of sanity. And the long procession of optimists who have risked humiliation to speak sweet reason in Baghdad and come back frustrated.

Last efforts at mediation followed each other like the positively final appearances of famous opera singers.

Those efforts were due to the general unwillingness to surrender to the state of mental and moral chaos in which the power of reason has no part.

In order not to be humiliated, Saddam finds it necessary to try to humiliate the world, all take and no give. Faced with such a situation, the best will in the world eventually shows signs of wear.

'No linkage,' state the Americans and the British, fearful lest a grain of rectitude be found concealed in Saddam's argument. The French, Soviets and Belgians remained less convinced. Jimmy Carter made a statement which shows how his clairvoyance and authority have increased since his presidency ended. First, he called for an international conference in lieu of military action and declared with honesty that there is linkage whether we like it or not.

The father of the Camp David agreement, that triumph of diplomacy, is certainly deserving of attention. Those so eager to refute linkage maintain that concern for the fate of the Palestinians was merely an afterthought in Saddam Hussein's mind, once he understood the strategic advantage of a holy war. It was, in other words, far from his mind when he walked into Kuwait as a rampant layman.

All this may well be so but, since the host of United Nations resolutions about the fate of the Palestinians remain unimplemented, whereas those concerning Iraq's invasion of Kuwait have brought in a huge armada, there is every justification for speaking of double standards. Once there are double standards there is, inevitably, linkage.

An international conference may well come up with results no more constructive than the present ugly impasse, but at least a subject of major concern to the future of every nation will have been ventilated.

And let no one sell the mere fact of ventilation short. There are those who equate the riots in the Soviet Baltic republics with the invasion of Hungary at the very moment of the Suez crisis. Certainly, the events in Lithuania are extremely depressing and President Gorbachev's explanation that he knew nothing of the military action until later was embarrassing to everyone once infected by his enthusiasm and novel thinking. In truth, there is no parallel between the Soviet Union then and now. Where, then, were the outraged reactions of Soviet parliamentarians? And where were the vestiges of a Lithuanian government?

It is easy to attribute the natural roughness of exasperated soldiery to the policy of a government. But we all remember the excesses of the National Guard on the campuses, the toughness of the French and British police during provocative strikes, the atrocities in South Africa; they shocked public opinion at first but then were accepted as the reflexes of a moment, not as a norm for future crowd control.

President Gorbachev is head of a huge conglomerate of peoples, all finding out the perils of freedom and making up the rules as they go along. But they are ventilated. They change their thinking, they quarrel and they apologise.

Not so Saddam Hussein. There is not the trace of even a draught under his door. He has known how to answer all questions before they are asked and how to make self-destruction an obedient and even a jolly business.

25–27 January 1991

A Time Out of Joint

I re-read my contribution to the *European* of 14 December without any sense of satisfaction. I wrote then: 'Even as far back as 1914 . . . the experts talked of "a war over by Christmas". Christmas 1914, that is. In 1939, the Germans launched what they called a Blitzkrieg. It started well enough for them, this lightning war, but finally became entangled in the undergrowth and dragged on endlessly, with enormous loss of life and human dignity.

'Now this ageing monster is being summoned from its slumbers yet again, with talk of a sudden, swift and surgical operation in the Gulf. That indispensable element of surprise, no doubt, which, before long, turns to surprise that the whole exercise should still be going on so long after the first rapid strike.'

Well, of course, the war has not been going on that long. It only seems long for the time being because it has hogged so much television prime-time. At first it was all nefariously exciting. But then it was revealed that the war on Cable News Network was Saddam Hussein's favourite viewing and the censors clamped down. Now we have as much time as before, devoted to television coverage of the war, but are mostly confronted by gallant if colourless general officers who tell us that they are unable to tell us what we want to know. It is up to us as individuals to find some kind of stimulation in this monotonous procedure.

There are, however, certain areas which cannot be easily subjected to censorship. Expenditure, for instance. The war is busy trying to find sponsors. Money is continually being sought in order to make this hideously expensive pastime possible. The Germans, it is felt, are not pulling their weight. Nor are the Japanese. But, since both countries were copiously punished for behaving just as Saddam Hussein is doing, only on a much larger scale and within living memory, they both have a natural access to reticence. They were both kept out of military affairs for so long that it made their industrial miracles possible. They consequently entered the modern world slightly ahead of the rest of us and now fob off any temptation to be lured back into obsolescence by making generous gifts of a billion here and a billion there.

The French awakened the usual suspicions in the Anglo-Saxon camp when they tried last-minute diplomacy. This ran counter to the diktat of 'no linkage'. If the British believe that they enjoy a special relationship with the United States (after all, they share a War of Independence), the French believe they have a special relationship with the Arab countries, for much the same reasons.

Not to understand such phenomena is to be insensitive to history and, therefore, to betray a melancholy incompetence in the understanding of the affairs of the Gulf. Those unable to understand will never be able to contribute much to the solutions of these age-old problems.

It is, of course, churlish to make too much of one's doubts while a war is in progress but, at the same time, it is a duty at least as compelling as loyalty to obey profound convictions. We are being invited – some of us are being ordered – to take a giant step backwards into that murky past of pride and prejudice from which we erroneously thought we had been freed for ever.

The clichés of combat are reappearing one by one. One American soldier, crouched beside his tank, replied, when asked what he thought about out in the desert, 'The red, white and blue. What else is there?'

Clearly a private soldier, winkled out by a journalist from back home, and responding to a question not lacking in inanity, will be tempted to say something calculated to give pleasure. But a patchwork of such quietly heroic platitudes, stretching through the day, tends to give an added feeling of unreality to a situation which already strains credulity.

There is nothing new in this, alas. The Crusaders are still present in spirit in the area, spreading their ferocious intolerance around for others to imitate in the name of God. The echo of the footfall of Roman legions still pervades the arid valleys. Before them, the great conflict between Babylon and Jerusalem with slings and arrows instead of Scuds and Patriots.

Then, later, the incompetent, loose-limbed and surprisingly tolerant regime of the Ottoman Turks, probably the regime which best suited the local mentality and allowed it to breathe. Finally, the casual arrogance of the western European powers and, eventually, the excitement and risks of independence. It has been a long history and there is little to suggest that it has been understood by those in power.

Mr Perez de Cuellar, normally a reticent, undemonstrative man, suggested on his return from Baghdad that Saddam might be well advised to see a psychiatrist. The weight of history can rest heavy on the mind. Meanwhile, President Bush complained that Saddam's behaviour was irrational. Well done – he noticed. And yet, to be irrational is to be in tune with the times.

1 February 1991

From Here to Eternity

For some, this may be the year of Bush, or yet of Major. To others it may well be the year of Saddam Hussein; even of Schwarzkopf. But if we raise our eyes from the fuss and fidget of the daily grind to the calming level of permanent values, this remains indelibly and importantly the year of Mozart. His contribution is behind him but it grows and renews itself with every passing day, an endless rediscovery, a smiling but unsentimental reaffirmation of human values. His mysteries are all accessible. Only when the works are over does it occur to us to ask by what magic such divine simplicity could have emerged from such a web of subtle complication.

Mozart may have been Austrian, as was Hitler. But both these artists were European, the more important of the two a glorious example of human possibility, the other a terrible warning of how a frustrated house painter can take it out on the landscape if allowed to. Both matured on the rich soil of Europe, the one destined for eternity, the other linked forever to his own time which he helped to make mournful, tragic and heroic, a final chapter of festering prejudices, a last surge of the gangrene in European history.

Both Hitler and President Bush spoke of a new order. They meant very different things. Mr Bush has a vision of a world balanced by a healthy interest in prosperity through inter-dependence, with the military might of the US in the background in case this message is misunderstood yet again by some miscreant.

Hitler was the miscreant of the time and merely wanted the world to know who was master. And where is Mozart in all this? He has survived all the passions of the moment and speaks to us in a voice which expresses, with startling clarity, the gamut of emotions from distress to defiance, from playfulness to solemnity. No shift of frontiers, no overthrow of regime has silenced his voice and it will be heard when all the yelling from the balconies and the pep talks to the boys have passed into the yellowing archives.

Another great lesson taught by Mozart is a wondrous sense of proportion, of balance. This is especially valuable at a moment when this ancient melting-pot of rich cultures called Europe is being invited by its ill-wishers to doubt its own possibility of cohesion. We are told by these pundits that the present peculiar situation has conclusively proved that, even if there is some reality to the economic community, it only takes what is termed an emergency to bring out the inadequacies in the entire project. Well, if Europe cannot yet respond to the call of duty it is perhaps because we can no longer understand what our duty is and, if there are doubts, these must be ventilated. A fanfare on a bugle or a ration of sophistry are no longer sufficient to impose an unquestioning silence on those with minds of their own who regard the use of the mind as a human right.

Efforts have been made to clarify our thinking for us. Saddam Hussein is the equivalent of Hitler, we are told. We were taught our lesson about appeasement at Munich; negotiation is but a less contentious name for appeasement. I hear the distant bugle, but need more convincing. Hitler was in charge of a huge and, for the times, ultra-modern military machine, able to think up its own weapons, to invent its own secrets. He was held at bay, heroically, by a handful of underdogs and the sheer imbalance in the conflict brought out the best in them.

Today, we have a large and technologically highly developed army, with practically endless resources, apart from cash flow, facing a bloated power living on its military capital. It is not the kind of war which fires the imagination. Especially if one side is attempting, quite rightly, to save the lives which are within the bounds of its responsibility. As for the others – other lives, that is – it is absolutely credible that Allied airmen are making every effort to spare the civilian population. Unfortunately, history judges the military not by what they aim at, but by what they hit. The facts about destruction live on, those about intentions are quickly forgotten. And an uneasy ambiguity hangs over the uncannily static scene. New peace initiatives break out. Gratuitous death is a vile occurrence, especially when there is time to think, and there is plenty of that, with the press straining for information and the powers-that-be reluctant to admit that very little is going on but insisting that the little is strictly according to plan.

Instead of blaming Europe for its variety of reactions to this strange situation, ill-wishers should have the generosity to admit that it is a miracle that the casus belli did not take place in Europe as it invariably has done in the past. We have moved beyond the world of frontiers at last. Mozart led the way. He has no need to fill up a form or make a declaration in order to be heard. And he can never be coveted as a possession, as he is at once the property of no one and of all. An eternal value.

8 February 1991

The World of Big Tips

I never thought I would live to hear US Secretary of State James Baker say that King Hussein of Jordan had changed sides. To make such an allegation is not to know the King, a privilege I have had for the best part of half a century. I was much less surprised to hear that the generous American grant to Jordan was being reconsidered as a punishment for a speech which seemed intemperate. Less surprised, because we live in the world of the big tipper, with sudden withdrawal of favour regularly used to censure the expression of unpopular opinion.

Remember, if you will, the declaration of the Yemeni chairman of the Security Council who dared to cast his vote against the motion condemning Iraq for the invasion of Kuwait. He said that his vote was a question of conscience, admitting that his gesture would no doubt mean the withdrawal of $70 million in American aid. The Egyptian debt for military hardware from the United States was wiped out as a gesture of gratitude for Egypt's willingness to be actively involved in the Gulf war. We can only guess at the deals with Syria and other countries, notably Israel, along the same lines.

Once governments behave in a manner which would entail instant arrest in individuals, and once the graceful term of enlightened self-interest is employed to justify the atmosphere of understated venality prevalent today, it strains credulity to accept President Bush's definition of the present conflict as one of good versus evil. That is strictly for the young of mind. Mark you, nothing that Mr Bush can say can make Saddam

Hussein's image less attractive than it already is, although it is absolutely possible that such a man may exert a certain charm on those who actually know him.

Hitler and Mussolini both exercised a peculiar magnetism on those who came across them before events had forced them into their respective corners. Saddam Hussein, backing towards his own corner, is certainly doing all he can to merit the sobriquet of evil.

From there to allege that good is the exclusive platform of the coalition is, however, far-fetched and even in doubtful taste. The massive and constant air attacks on military targets obviously make a great deal of strategic sense, even if they sicken the sensibilities of those who remember Dresden and even London during the Blitz. And the promise to reconstruct Iraq when it is all over is but a premonition of guilty conscience in those about to indulge in slaughter.

It is tragic than an outlaw living in the past should cause nations concentrating their energies on present and future to go back in time in order to accommodate his outmoded predilection for pitched battle. 'The mother of all battles?' And Saddam is, I suppose, the proud husband left holding the baby.

Mr De Klerk, in his historic speech to the South African parliament, equated the end of apartheid with the end of sanctions. This can only mean that sanctions had hurt South Africa, an item worthy of record. At the same time, the sanctions against South Africa were not for a moment as watertight as those against Iraq.

Adjoining countries depending on trade with South Africa were spared from joining in, a form of fundamental understanding never extended to Jordan.

Who can ever know whether the sanctions against Iraq might have done the trick and rendered the whole massive scenario redundant? No one. All we know is that weapons work a treat and I suppose that is some kind of relief. And what will happen when the scenario, eagerly written by so many contributors and controlled by so few, is finally at an end?

The great peace conference, the return of goodwill and golden handshakes for the deserving, the Palestinians represented by delegates of our choice. This is tantamount to Britain, during the American War of Independence, deciding to negotiate with the colonists on condition that their delegate was Benedict Arnold. The conflict may really only begin at the peace conference, even though the war is behind us. But meanwhile, let us applaud Germany which has even-handedly extended aid to Israel and Jordan as though it were her responsibility.

And let us wonder why the United States should have allowed her pique with the most liberal spirit in the region, who is merely expressing the opinion of his subjects, to cloud her magnanimity. It may be tough, but it is neither fair nor wise and, therefore, out of character.

15 February 1991

Pride and Prejudice

During a recent sojourn in Cologne, I was asked by a German parliamentarian what the reason was behind the resurgence of British militarism. My surprise at such a question was slightly diminished by the fact that it was not the first time I had been asked it. One must understand, of course, that the doctrine of pacifism as common-sense, rather than as idealism, is more deeply ingrained in the German nature than in that of practically any other nation.

They have seen it all, in their parlours, their backyards and cellars: war, occupation, humiliation, chaos, and they still carry with them a deep and, by now indefinable, guilt for the horrible excesses of the past – a guilt which the more objective of them feel they must at long last come to terms with.

The young tend to run a mile from all things military which seem hideous echoes from an authoritarian past. Families were so impregnated by misery and silenced by remorse that the nation has learned to live without an enemy. Their present prosperity, as well as a certain lack of scruples as to whom they do business with, may well be by-products of this emancipated state of mind, although the sale of weapons is by no means a German monopoly.

Britain, for so long the voice of reason, even historically that of appeasement, has been initially reluctant, but finally dogged, during both world wars from which she emerged temporarily dishevelled, impoverished, but victorious. For her, pacifism was always the solution of the impractical dreamer, an absence of realism in a world largely peopled by unpredictable and often treacherous foreigners.

And, despite universal progress in the direction of the ultimate common-sense, in which the innate intelligence and goodwill of peoples could be used to their mutual advantage by destroying the harmful prejudices which grow like weeds if left unchecked, there has been no shortage of incidents to remind Britain of her imperial past.

First, it was Iceland. Britain has always idealized herself as a small island, defying disproportionate continental powers. This struggle against an even smaller island, with a population less than half that of Bristol, hardly seemed adequate to tug at the deeper strings of patriotism. Yet one was astonished at the dark sonorities generated and at the stridency of the press.

Then came the Falklands, and the rallying cry of Mrs Thatcher which could hardly have been bettered by the first Elizabeth. For what it was, it was skilfully handled, caused tragic loss of life and some of the ugliest rhetoric since 'Hang the Kaiser'.

And now the Gulf. It is characteristic of wars that they bring out the worst in both sides. Whatever beastliness is perpetrated by one, it is sooner or later matched by the other. This adventure is no exception. One side is on television round the clock, unable to say much but saying it with pride and with an unwavering belief in the infallibility of our intelligence services and our superior technology. For 'our', read 'coalition'. For 'coalition', read 'American'. General Schwarzkopf, speaking about a truck which had just hurried past the graticule of an aimed missile on video: 'And meanwhile, in the rear-view mirror . . .' Explosion. Laughter. The atmosphere is agreeable, one might almost say civilised.

The British attitude to all this? The special relationship is what it has always been: an avuncular one, observing the American nephew with considerable

A RESURGENCE OF BRITISH MILITARISM?

affection and admiration. And certainly the very direct American approach to patriotism, utterly fearless of unrestrained sentimentality or tinsel, has fired the British uncle with fond memories of his heyday. 'We don't want to fight, but by jingo if we do . . .'

Every effort is being made to elevate the present crisis from the level of an elaborate punitive expedition to that of a third great war which deserves total loyalty and the unquestioning application of every citizen. At the beginning of all this, a hapless American general was removed from his command because he inadvertently claimed that the main war aim was the elimination of Saddam Hussein. Now the climate is sufficiently degraded for many to be expressing such an unconstitutional heresy, and President Bush has even incited the Iraqis themselves to rise against what he called the 'dictator'.

American generals said they could not guarantee the safety of an Iraqi civil airliner carrying Tariq Aziz to

Moscow. The punitive expedition has degenerated to this point.

The British obviously cannot match such dark ambitions so, for the time being, *mein Herr*, they do what they can to stoke the fires of antiquity by little diversions, like meretricious twaddle about the comportment of the British Royal Family. That is not enough, *mein Herr*, to make you fear British overstatement as a secret weapon of the future. It is merely a passing epidemic, like nearly everything else.

22 February 1991

Veto Power Abused

It is generally accepted that Saddam Hussein's army has been badly mauled and rendered groggy by incessant air attacks. It is also known, although less generally admitted, that Saddam has made his mark on the travel plans and airlines of the West. Large corporations slide perilously close to backruptcy, workers are laid off, shining examples to the muscle-men and other playboys of the Western world, like Rambo, cancel skiing holidays. And anyone in my shoes, who is obligated to write a weekly, as opposed to a daily, column in a newspaper, will recognise that Saddam is about as irritating as a mosquito on a summer's night. How can one guess what the fellow's going to be up to from moment to moment?

George Bush is utterly predictable by comparison. He evidently regards his own inflexibility as an act of faith towards deeply held beliefs. The only change, once we accept the notion that combatants invariably influence each other, is a sudden mysticism which compels him to announce to the Queen of Denmark (of all people) that every generation has its battle against the enemies of freedom. One hopes that he is wrong, simply because such a belief would justify the development of even more terrible weapons to decimate the future ranks of those who happen to be born in the wrong place.

Compared to the melancholy constancy of President Bush, Saddam is a wild improviser who evidently sees himself as an instant ayatollah, a warlord from the pages of the history books and a peace-loving family man, all at the same time. All this puts even schizophrenia under an unnatural strain and, whereas one is at times forced to admire glimmers of lucidity in the lunacy, the basic premise for his actions is inhuman and outmoded.

Whether the acrobatic mentality of one man justifies the deplacement of a huge armada will always be open to debate. The thing could certainly have been avoided if suppliers of military equipment had insisted on payment in cash, but it is too late for that now. The fact is that an army far greater than one needed for defence, but possessing weapons many of which are threatened with obsolescence, lies straddled over the landscape. The stage is set for carnage.

In order to justify this, the United Nations has been re-animated and a series of resolutions, by now variously interpreted, are brandished by the members of the so-called Alliance. Certainly the degree of consultation has been very high and the telephone between the concerned capitals is in practically constant use.

However, it is already becoming a pernicious habit to conduct meetings of the Security Council in closed session, which means that we have to rely on leakage by various ambassadors for information about the ebb and flow of the debate. At moments, the whole operation looks like an effort momentarily to hijack this vital forum of opinion in the interest of untroubled cohesion in the Alliance.

This is not what the United Nations was meant for by its founding fathers who were permitted a degree of idealism by the black night from which they had all emerged nearly half a century ago, and by the sudden impact of peace. But even they had an unhealthy respect for power and built the dubious weapon of the veto into the structure of their new creation.

This weapon has been abused quite as often as it has been used. Once UN Secretary-General Perez de Cuellar's voice is heard, as though muffled from a cupboard, usually expressing hope where we have already been informed by engaged authorities that there is none, it would seem that in a situation requiring clairvoyance about the type of peace which will emerge after the end of this tragic interlude, the General Assembly is a more equitable arena for the ventilation of world opinion than the hothouse of the Security Council.

Kuwait already lies bleeding while Western commercial interests jockey for position in the subsequent battle for its reconstruction. But this matters less than the issues before the peacemakers which will be entirely different from the narrow aims of war. The only similarity will be the predominance of influential nations, eager discreetly to assume the continuance of their ability to influence, and the clamour of the have-nots, those under-privileged by nature, who export labour rather than oil.

And in the background, the contributions of those less actively engaged in local realities, yet interested by virtue of race, creed, trade or even morality, in a world still far too clearly divided between the haves and the have-nots, a permanent reason for insecurity. It used to be said that every war was fought with the weapons of the last one. If only this were true. Technology has made such advances, often at the expense of decency, that every war is fought with the mentality of the last one but with weapons which can be best described as state-of-the-art. An ugly phrase to describe ugly things.

1 March 1991

The Harder Challenge

The Gulf war is over. According to both sides, both sides have won and, therefore, both sides must have lost too. Undeniably, there has been a colossal victory and a colossal defeat. Saddam Hussein was never one to be content with walking tall; he felt safer on stilts. Now that these have been cut down to size, he seems to have disappeared. Perhaps they are just searching for him at the wrong level.

To the rest of us, reduced by circumstances to the role of spectators, it feels as though we had listened to an interminable overture with the lights dimmed and, when the curtain eventually rose, the opera itself lasted a few paltry minutes of intolerable noise.

Of course, the critics agree, it has been a tremendous technical achievement, this business of co-ordinating the actions of thousands of performers on a relatively small stage without them getting in each other's way too often. Apart from a consensus about the pyrotechnics, there are those who feel that this short work is a breakthrough to new horizons and others who believe it to be pretty poor stuff.

There are as many opportunities in life to be amazed by the physical courage of the human animal under stress as there are causes to be depressed by a general shortage of moral courage. The testimony of ordinary warriors is unfailingly moving, often expressed with a kind of fatalistic humour and simplicity which both disarms and warms the heart, perhaps because it seeks to influence no one.

I invariably feel the opinions of leaders to be much more suspect, no doubt because they seek to convince

NEW STATUE PROJECT FOR GATES OF BAGHDAD (TO SCALE)

and to propagate that elusive quality which they themselves think of as leadership. Leadership can be inspired at times. It can also be workaday – moments without inspiration, moments of rhetoric.

All the actors in this drama are becoming daily more interesting. Take Mikhail Gorbachev, for instance. He is a prime example of one who displays evident moral courage when the issues are clear. To reach his present eminence within the Soviet state, he went about his civilizing and ventilating task with incredible energy and absolute clarity of mind. He knew exactly what had to be done and he did it.

Inevitably, he reached a stage of success at which the issues were no longer clear and it would have been inhuman to expect him to see so far into the unknown future. Now he tends to disapppoint even his most devoted followers simply because the events he created have taken on a life of their own and the many voices he invited to speak do not necessarily agree with him. In a way, it is the unavoidable friction between a father's hopes and the reality of his children's personalities.

George Bush has also changed considerably, at least to the distant observer. All the time the conflict threatened and slowly became a fact, practically the only constant note to be struck was the somewhat sallow inflexibility of the White House, reiterated hundreds of times like the dullest of thuds.

Now that the dragon in Baghdad is confined to quarters rather than slain, a new and infinitely touching George Bush is emerging, one who suddenly chooses to abandon all the comforting platitudes one half expects from those in high office. Ronald Reagan may have been the great communicator, which has its advantages, though its principal drawback is that the communication remains, at all times, a performance.

George Bush goes further by rejecting all facility, daring to dramatize his doubts and even to give us a

precious inkling of his torments. He could not share in the euphoria, he said. It may be possible later, he hinted, but at this time . . .

He recognizes, of course, that a phase is at an end. There have been deaths, fewer than expected, but, as always, more than there should have been. A one-sided battle is never enjoyable. In the words of a GI, it was like 'taking candy from a baby'. It seemed necessary at the time, with all the talk of gas and bacteriological capabilities, but it wounds the self-esteem of the victorious. There is nothing worse for the morale than an unequal battle.

But now the real challenge begins. Wisdom cannot be improved by technological means and single-mindedness is no longer sufficient. George Bush seems willing to expose his deepest misgivings to the scrutiny and contemplation of those who look to him as their commander-in-chief and that is the most hopeful symptom of the new-found peace. It simply means that he listens as well as talks – a great compliment to the American people and not easy for the first citizen of a country which has resumed walking tall.

A final word of appreciation for General Schwarzkopf, a most untypical military man, who has given not only lucidity, but even corpulence, a kind of radiance. And an admonition in anticipation of the eventual peace conference.

I give you an ancient Chinese proverb I made up the other day while reflecting on nations and their complexes: 'He who walk tall no see where put foot.'

8 March 1991

Mistaken Comeback

A curious epoch. The battle is over. Peace has been declared. The boys are on their way home. The fighting goes on. Rather like the end of a boxing match, one would say. After long rounds of observation, with left jabs against practically no opposition, and a public growing restless, the sudden release of a series of piled-rivers; the smaller boxer lies on the ground, momentarily inanimate, while the victor gives interviews and waves reassuringly at his supporters.

Meanwhile, many onlookers invade the ring. No one knows anyone else's function or even identity, and it is presumed that they all have some reason to be there. Only the victor is eager to go back to the changing room and think of other things.

Other things? One had almost forgotten the exit of Mrs Thatcher from the scene or the seemingly mild but trenchant speech of Sir Geoffrey Howe, that extraordinary day in the United Kingdom Parliament, when his delivery was as demure as his meaning was crystal clear. There followed a few more snarls of defiance and then the sudden realization that the game was up. The actual departure was beautifully judged and invested with just the right mix of truculence and good humour to make it memorable. As always in life, there is nothing like a disaster to bring out the true dimension of the victim. It was one of the most remarkable leave-takings of our time.

One of the great rules of the theatre is that, once you have gained your applause, you must not come back under the impression that the public is demanding an encore instead of merely marking its appreciation.

Unfortunately, and embarrassingly, the lady is back, having heard the applause at the end of the war and believing that she deserved to remind the public of her share in victory.

Not content with taking a curtain call and accepting a bouquet from George Bush himself (undoubtedly deserved) she decided to make her views known as though they were not known already. It is rare that a person of such sure instincts should fall into such a trap. One had become so grateful for her silence, at least for a while.

She not only castigated her colleagues for their inability to share her lack of popularity at a given moment, but made it seem as though a lack of popularity in some mysterious way proves the rightness of a cause. This is surely a dangerous assumption in a democracy. If people become sufficiently unpopular, they usually go, which she had the grace to do.

And once she had invoked democracy, she boasted that the British Parliament is 700 years old whereas Germany's is only forty, Spain's a dozen years old and Portugal's even less. What a peculiar criterion this is. Iceland's parliament is even older than the British one and I don't remember this fact being mentioned during the Cod War.

Rebuking some European nations, who refused to send troops to help the coalition war effort, Mrs Thatcher claimed that we were prepared to risk life to uphold liberty. She had hoped that Europe was prepared to do the same. It was not.

Who was prepared to risk life, pray? Who is this collective 'we' but those in power who send young professionals to theatres of conflict? That may be part of their mandate, but it is surely tasteless to suggest that they do other than risk lives not their own. There seems no limit to the presumption of politicians.

One remembers Churchill's wartime conclusion that Poland should take two steps to the left. It was a very cryptic end to difficult negotiations but nobody thought at the time of the untold agony of such a decision: thousands of ethnic Poles finding themselves within the Soviet Union, thousands of Germans finding themselves in Poland. Evidently, it is in the nature of high office that it precludes the exercise of undue sensitivity and that, at times, decency must be relegated to the province of oratory.

Nobody seeks to denigrate the gallantry of the British armed forces or the doggedness of the civilian population. I am old enough to know; older than Mrs Thatcher. But to refer to Britain's unique historical heritage as an excuse for opposing an alleged German domination of Europe is merely a sentimental and retrogressive attitude miserably out of tune with the temper of our times.

There is no domination in Europe. The only risk of domination resides in the disunity of Europe within its old pattern of frontiers and alliances.

The English had a great deal of trouble at one point in the bad old days from Joan of Arc. This young foreign lady heard voices and therefore lacked the lucidity of Mrs Thatcher, who only seems to hear one voice: her own.

15 March 1991

Beware the Sly Surgeon

Compare, if you will, the different techniques employed by the opposing parties in the recent conflict. The diplomacy of the Alliance was virtually non-existent. In fact, any trace of private initiatives in the wings of the Security Council was severely censured – Mr Bush and his followers remained entrenched in their position of inflexible moral rectitude. The military thinking of the same group was ingenious, flexible and ultimately dazzling.

In Iraq, the military was as inflexible as was Allied diplomacy. But the Iraqi military used every device known or unknown in the field of public relations in its battle for public opinion before hostilities actually broke out. Well, we all know who won. We also know that it is not over yet. King Hussein of Jordan is invariably described as a great survivor, but his quality is that of a serene religious fatalism coupled with a quiet integrity.

Compared to this muted nobility, Saddam Hussein is a consummate improviser, a man with the temperament of a confidence trickster who conjures inspiration out of thin air and becomes the first and willing victim of his own eloquence. He evidently trusts implicitly the voice of his wayward muse. He believes every word he utters, not after he has thought it but after he hears himself say it.

The long war with Iran seemed to contain and finally curb the ambitions of a certain kind of reckless religious fundamentalism, and the future Allies were grateful for what appeared to be a dose of secular sanity in that part of the world. Weapons were even sold to Saddam

Hussein at illusory profits. When that war ended, we were all as grateful as we were appalled by the start of the new adventure.

For the invasion of Kuwait, Saddam deemed it unnecessary to change his character from that of the energetic National Socialist folk hero, every inch a layman. It was only later, when he felt the need to inspire international subversion as his ally, that he became deeply religious overnight, crying aloud for a jihad, a holy war. Now he was frequently photographed on his knees, lowering his forehead to the ground and wearing an expression of atonement on his face. The change was perhaps a mite too quick and expedient to convince even the most gullible of mullahs. The fact is that the cry for a holy war failed to penetrate even the outer fabric of the Alliance.

Now, in the prevailing chaos, the aftermath of defeat, he comes up with something new and daring: democracy. It is not as though he had just discovered it. He had been on the point of making great and radical changes in Iraqi society when he was rudely interrupted by the unprovoked Allied invasion. There is apparently no end to the capacity for self-delusion enjoyed by this ingenious malefactor.

It would not be too surprising to hear that, when democracy eventually comes to Iraq, every voter will be accorded two votes, making the country twice as democratic as any other by Saddam's reckoning.

But meanwhile the Alliance, moderately scrupulous in its interpretation of the Security Council Resolution in time of war, has become utterly scrupulous in time of armistice. Any hint of military occupation, any suspicion of colonial powers acting out of force of habit is anathema in this day and age. The Allies stop at the edge of the arena and watch the carnage, their reputation unsullied. Considering the way in which comparisons between Saddam and Hitler were freely

146

bandied about by the War Party before the conflict, it is quite in order to ask these eager people whether they would have been in favour of halting the Allied war effort just within the confines of Germany, allowing Hitler to head a new government while the SS was shooting refugees in the countryside.

The pressure to bring the lads home is more than understandable, but the present confusion in Iraq is militating in Saddam's favour. Strong men are in their element in times of trouble and the likelihood of those struggling to survive finding an alternative grows slimmer with every passing day. As contagion threatens a land deprived of energy and water, it is time to unleash the floodgates of medical and technical aid once again through the agencies of the United Nations. Generosity and compassion will do more to overthrow the dictator than studied indifference.

It will draw attention to his responsibility for the tragedy. But beware lest he turns up in medical garb, having just done a crash course in surgery and having awarded himself a professorship, just to be in step with the times.

22 March 1991

Old Men in the Dock

The timing is almost unbelievable. At the very moment when those of normal sensibility are still horrified by the fact that the six men incarcerated for the bombing of the Birmingham pubs have spent sixteen long years in prison for no valid reason, other evidence having come to light to cast more than a question over the validity of their arrest in the first place, Parliament is willing to resume its pursuit of alleged war criminals living in Britain.

The first time the Bill was presented to the House of Lords, it was thrown out. Now it comes up for a second reading before that controversial House, with a few dire threats which might force the acquiescence of the Lords to the wishes of the Commons.

There is considerable pressure to persuade Lord Lane, the Lord Chief Justice, to resign for his responsibility in what is regarded as a miscarriage of justice. He was a member of the Appeal Court which rejected the Birmingham Six's appeal for a retrial. He is now seventy-three years old. At a time when the majority of war crimes were committed, he would have been in his mid-twenties. If we admit that, in order to be responsible for giving orders to commit a war crime, a culprit would have to be in a relatively senior position, it is unlikely that any surviving war criminal would today be much under the age of eighty. This would have made him a person in his early thirties at the time of his criminal activity, which is just credible.

But if the criminals are now in their eighties, so are the witnesses. What memories are reliable, or free from prejudice, at that age? Can the will to tell the truth really be detached from the desire to please, to be helpful? And where is the dignity in bringing a doddering octogenarian before mortal justice, only to risk having death cheat the spirit of revenge while due process takes its own majestic time?

Is it not possible that the unexpectedly wide divergence of opinion between the majorities in the lower and the upper House is due to the fact that the average age in the Lords is considerably higher than that in the Commons, and that the venerable aristocracy has the grace to acknowledge the danger of waning powers and indistinct recollections in those resting on winter laurels, whereas the younger generations have hardly any cause to stretch their compassion to such lengths?

Certainly, the pursed lips of Kenneth Baker, Home Secretary, which seem to reflect some secret satisfaction in their subtle curl, frequently part to admonish the dotards that no further hesitation will be tolerated. Justice, he implies, must be done, up to the very gates of the mortuary. What justice?

The Nuremberg Trials were laid on very suspect foundations: a retrospective legislation, seeking to combine the legal systems of the United States, Britain, France and Stalin's Soviet Union in a single cohesive and lucid structure.

Such a hybrid is certainly more able to condemn than to give doubt its benefit. Rudolf Hess's tragi-farcical end, keeping a huge prison in existence by virtue of his inability to die, was the direct result of an impasse between the more forgiving West and Soviet obtuseness.

The kidnapping of Eichmann was fine *Boy's Own* comic stuff; more palatable as fiction than as fact. Naturally, the world understood the Jewish desire for retribution at the time as a natural reaction to the most ambitious and revolting act of genocide in history. But kidnapping cannot be condoned as a means of settling accounts. It is terrorism pure and simple, however just the outcome may appear.

This method evidently rubbed off on the French when they tricked Barbie out of his South American fastness and made him stand trial in Lyon. This trial was labelled fair, although a monument to the deportation was unveiled in front of the courthouse on the very day of its inception, raising the climate of emotions during the proceedings.

Barbie infuriated the French authorities by grabbing at the few crumbs of dignity at his disposal and refusing to leave his cell. The trial was certainly motivated by a lofty desire for justice, but its effect was anti-climactic and its reflection on human nature depressing.

Since then, other efforts to bring old men to the dock have been characterized by doubts as to their true identity, while among others Baby Doc Duvalier and Idi Amin live out a dignified retirement.

Is it not time for the human race to remember the virtues of clemency? And are not double standards one too many? At all events, it is better that the innocent go free after sixteen years of incarceration than that the guilty escape mortal justice after half a century of furtive liberty.

29 March 1991

Worst of All Worlds

Remember *The Tortoise and the Hare*, Aesop's fable about the race between two animals? The hare was so evidently the faster that he was carried away by the ease of his imminent victory and allowed himself to be distracted within sight of the finishing post, leaving the single-minded tortoise to crawl by and win.

Are we not witnessing an epic re-enactment of this morality tale, with a cast of millions? Schwarzkopf the Hare streaked towards an overwhelming victory when halted in his tracks by orders from above. Saddam the Tortoise struggled on and is now just about level with the day-dreaming hare. Victory is still in sight for both.

Where is the remotest logic in all this? Does the unbelievable anomaly of the present situation reside in the unrequited desire of the United States to be loved as well as respected? Is the US suddenly so sensitive to charges of interfering in the internal affairs of other nations that it is prepared to abandon the inflexibility of the past for this extraordinary volte-face?

Frankly, if this was to be the result, the whole high-tech adventure of the Gulf War should never have taken place at all. Is it all the result of a kind of inexperience, this business of judging others by the norms pertaining at home? Certainly, in most countries, a disaster on the scale of the Iraqi military humiliation would have entailed an immediate change of government, but was it wise to presume that there were no exceptions to this rule? And is it honourable to encourage the opponents of the regime to rise up against Saddam and to decline to answer their appeals for help once they have taken up the few arms at their disposal?

It all seemed so clear-cut before the war broke out. The mandate was to free Kuwait. Now Kuwait is free once more and seen in a fairly unappealing light as the arbitrary persecution of Palestinians continues on the basis of nationality rather than culpability, and the medieval rulers are rejoined emotionally with their jewelled saddles and stretched limousines.

The matter is complicated by the fact that Britain and France laid the tables for this ongoing banquet and are responsible at least for the place settings. Kuwait, as such, is marked on older maps as a city, not as a state. It became that during my lifetime, despite its veneer of feudal antiquity, a somewhat suspect result of British prescience.

The Kurds, that tragic people spread over several recognized countries, were guaranteed their local autonomy by the Treaty of Sèvres in 1920. But this agreement was conveniently ignored by Turkey, Iran, Iraq, Syria and the Soviet Union, the five nations over which Kurdistan extends.

The rich oilfields of Mossul were confiscated from the Turks by the British after the First World War as a penalty for having fought on the side of the Germans, while the region of Alexandretta was lopped off Syria and given to the Turks by the French during the Second World War as a reward for not having made the same mistake again.

It will no doubt be appreciated that the West Bank, the Gaza Strip and the Golan Heights are not the only bones of territorial contention in a particularly febrile part of our planet.

To muddy the waters even further, the sudden revelation of President Saddam Hussein as one of the world's great capitalists, even having holdings in such unlikely publications as *Car and Driver* through his share in Hachette, has excited the Kuwaitis to seek reparations from the estimated $10 billion nest-egg.

THE EMIR OF KUWAIT

BEFORE THE WAR

DURING THE WAR

AFTER THE WAR

The initial American enthusiasm for the idea is somewhat dampened, we are told, by the British and the French, who deemed that such action might cause dangerous dislocations in the business world. It is as though exploratory surgery had revealed an ugly cancer in the affairs of men which the experts declare to be beyond repair. There is nothing to do but stitch the patient up again and change the subject.

Meanwhile, poor brilliant Schwarzkopf, the Hare, has already described his boss's decision to call a halt as courageous, no doubt a tactful way of saying something rather less flattering. He also called the decision humane. A curious choice of word to use in the context of the present civil war. More than 100,000 men, women, and children will have died for no reason at all. And it is not over yet.

The Allies' casualties were mercifully extremely light but how many will be willing to risk their lives the next

153

time, when told that the conflict is one of good against evil, once we see the usual collusion between good and evil in the worst of both worlds?

5 April 1991

What Price Freedom?

It is touching in the extreme that every nation believes itself to be the freest in the world. 'The land of the free!' belts out the patriotic American baseball crowd, as if there were no others. The British console themselves with the illusion that everything in the domain of freedom enjoyed by the Americans derives from Britain.

The French concept of liberty is shouted from the barricades. It is truculent, delirious and resolutely anarchic. Even the Russians, under Big Brother Stalin, sang a jaunty popular song which included the words 'I know of no other land where man can breathe as freely.'

Obviously, liberty is a normal aspiration for civilized man. Democracy, the outward expression of liberty organized along feasible lines, needs a degree of sophistication in its application. Compared with mere *laissez-faire* existence, it is the framework within which people may agree to differ and the majority of laws are obeyed for a specific period, though not in silence.

The question, unresolved after centuries of history, is how much freedom is compatible with the efficient running of a government? Here we run into a multitude of different solutions, some of them permanently unsatisfactory, perhaps because those in charge of national security always find it difficult to distinguish between opinion and subversion. Opinion is sacrosanct; in fact, it is the fuel which guarantees the smooth functioning of democracy. Subversion is quite the opposite – an attempt at disruption.

Let me give you an example. A Swiss social worker, active in helping the Third World, acquired his personal dossier from the authorities, dossiers having recently become available on request. He found he was suspect because he had once had lunch with a member of the Cuban embassy.

He could remember neither the menu nor the motive, only that the official was a charming lady. This fact was evidently not mentioned in the dossier. It never is. All this leads one to the British and French passion for secrecy. The French have even coined the deliberately mysterious phrase *raison d'état*. Sometimes secrecy must be necessary and this phrase puts the interests of the state above those of truth and honesty, under certain circumstances, but it is, by its very nature, open to abuse.

The lamentable incident of the sabotage of the Greenpeace boat in New Zealand was a case in point where the curtain was momentarily lifted on a classic *raison d'état* in action, and it was found to be a failure and stupid to boot.

The absurd saga of Peter Wright's book, *Spycatcher*, was another case in point. Every effort was made by the British Government to stifle the book at birth, on the grounds of a binding oath taken by secret agents never to divulge confidential material. The British authorities, who believed their strictures to be applicable the world over, suffered a rude awakening in the Australian courts where Lord Armstrong, the then head of the Civil Service in London, coined an immortal phrase by admitting that he had been 'economical with the truth'.

American society is, by its very nature, far more porous than most of its European counterparts. Leaks are the order of the day as are unauthorized and scandalous biographies published by reputable publishing houses. Rumour is rife at all times and disinformation, while rarely a fine art, is at least a common practice. There is more negotiation attached to verdicts in criminal cases than is the custom elsewhere and it leads one to the belief that Judas was about the first plea-bargainer in history.

What is clear is that a venerable figure like Dr Samuel Johnson would immediately acquire a dossier in most police archives today for having said, in a moment of thunderous clairvoyance, that patriotism is the last refuge of the scoundrel. Such a sentiment is even more suspect than lunch with a Cuban diplomat to the kind of minds which open dossiers.

Clemenceau was prime minister when he remarked that war is too serious a business to be left to the military. Had he been a humble citizen, or even out of office, his opinion would have immediately sounded subversive rather than penetratingly objective.

It takes the fulgurant French to find a phrase to fit the recurring anomalies. Oh Liberty, Liberty, how many crimes have been committed in your name? Pass us the dossier and we'll start counting. One thing we can tell you without even a glance at the record – the most recent crime is being committed at this moment.

12 April 1991

Power of the People

There are two vital lessons to be learned from the recent events in the Gulf which seem bound to influence the future of public affairs in a drastic fashion. One of these lessons, which has evidently not yet been digested by our leaders, is the fact that, since the events of the day are covered by television and by a press rendered extremely vigilant by this competition, not only are we all participants in the unfolding of events but also subject to rapid and intelligent editorials. The result of this phenomenon is a much faster crystallization of public opinion than before.

This change would probably pass unnoticed if it were not for the apparent inability of our leaders to assimilate the new situation. An example: President Bush is still thanking God that Kuwait is free and stating with vehemence that he will not intervene militarily in what is referred to as the internal affairs of Iraq, a politician's manner of avoiding a mention of the Kurds.

The fact is that Kuwait is a state of recent manufacture, conjured out of the desert for the benefit of oil interests, whereas the Kurds are an ancient people with their own language and their own culture, often promised autonomy by the Western powers but still, after centuries, awaiting the fulfilment of these pious commitments.

Ironically, it was only the triumphal, if abrupt, end of the war to liberate Kuwait which signalled the uprising of the Kurds, inspired by pamphlets dropped from the air urging desertion from the Iraqi army and other acts of insurrection. These pamphlets, seen by a French parliamentary mission in northern Iraq, can only have been dropped by American aircraft and led no doubt to the continuing assertion that the Kurds had been encouraged to rise and then denied all the help they had the right to expect.

The official American line, at the time adhered to by the British and French, was that the war was now over since the mandate of the United Nations had been fulfilled. This was a statement which, as yet, has taken no account of the groundswell of public opinion, fuelled by films and still photographs of unsurpassed horror, showing the helter-skelter flight of the Kurds to avoid massacre.

The day afterwards, United Kingdom Prime Minister John Major made a statement outside No 10 Downing Street, assuring the nation that blankets and medical supplies were on their way. He added, somewhat gratuitously, that he did not recollect having asked the Kurds to rise up. This sounded like a strangely inapposite echo of some obscure colonial heritage still hovering in the corridors of power.

Mr Major should perhaps have known better, as should Mr Bush when he paid his compliment to the particular value of American lives, of which, as we know, mercifully few were lost. Both remarks were probably intended for the satisfaction of internal markets, but everything uttered these days is carried to the four corners of the earth. Lesson number two. Nothing said or done has a purely local significance any more. Every life is valuable, every loss of it is tragic. There is no Dow Jones by which to judge life's value, even in the process of running for election.

Very quickly, the tidal wave of public concern and outrage began to alter the opinions of those in the driving seats who had thought, no doubt, they could get away with mere assurances that something would be done. Now, they are setting up zones within Iraq in which succour can be given to the hordes of refugees.

Long may the pressure continue because it is real democracy at work – not merely the votes of the elected but the palpable anger of the electorate reflected in pertinent and passionate editorials.

We live at the beginning of an era of total participation of public opinion in the process of government. Television has played an enormous part in this change, as has the press. This will inevitably affect the secrecy of public affairs and the luxury of time wasted in reaching decisions. Already, in Britain and France, there are soul-searching investigations into the nature of justice and the ability of the law to reflect this elusive ideal. It is all part of the same process, one of clarification, demystification, of honesty.

Politics, as witness the diminishing turn-outs at election times, is often discredited. The process is subject to public scrutiny on television. The climate of opinion is endlessly and immediately variable.

Unless those responsible for our destinies recognize the extraordinary speed of popular reactions in this age of information, they will increasingly give the impression of being out of touch, of concealing the truth and of playing for time. At their peril.

19 April 1991

Enchanting Celebrations

Rarely can any septuagenarian have been given such a birthday. Enough has already been written about it in these pages to make my remarks brief in the interests of good taste. However, to say it was overwhelming is a mean-minded understatement. Who, celebrating the attainment of any age, could dream of two still very active political leaders, not at the helm of their governments as in the past, but now in even hotter seats – at the grand piano?

Even traditional opponents of their policies would have had to agree that they played extremely well. In the case of Helmut Schmidt, it was some very free variations of *Happy Birthday to You*, reminiscent of Beethoven in Scottish mood but, more likely, vintage Schmidt. Ted Heath rendered *For He's a Jolly Good Fellow* with a broad Handelian sweep which befits his florid appearance and that very English characteristic of boisterous plain speaking expressed with an inherent shyness.

There were many other unforgettable moments: the exquisite tenderness of Sir Yehudi Menuhin's duet with Montserrat Caballé in a song by Richard Strauss, and the contained felinity of the latter as she purred her way through Rossini's aria for two cats with Barbara Hendricks. However, to pick out individual contributors to this extraordinary celebration is to be unfair to all those there is neither time nor space to mention. Suffice it to say that I was particularly enchanted by the contributions of those older than myself, like that German veteran, Heinz Rühmann, now approaching his ninetieth birthday with an exemplary serenity.

It was all far more than I deserved. But once there was to be such an extravagance, I am doubly grateful for the fact that it took place in surroundings dedicated to science, education and culture. The founding fathers of the United Nations dreamed up this tribute to man's inherent optimism and very properly placed it in Paris. It had to be located in a climate where it is possible to talk of culture without apologising for the word and Paris fits such a condition all too well.

Unesco would have been ill at ease in either New York or London and, in fact, those two influential powers are not at this time represented by ambassadors for reasons which may have had a certain validity a long time ago, but which appear pretty specious today.

Mark you, there may have been a constitutional error at the outset in that matters of the spirit should not really be relegated to ambassadors, however flattering it may have seemed at the beginning to mark the organization's importance by such considerations. Past experiences have shown that this diplomatic link merely causes the frictions and prejudices of the General Assembly and Security Council to be reflected in this world of cultural exchange, and that is the last influence it needs.

When the rift occurred, causing the withdrawal of the US ambassador, it was basically due to a personality clash with the then director-general who was accused of militating on behalf of Third World countries who desired their own news agencies.

This was regarded as an effort to control the news at source, thereby dictating to public opinion in those places. All this might have been convincing if the truth were a pristine value recognized by all, above and beyond the ebb and flow of regional and local opinion. But, of course, news is today tendentious by its very nature and the editorials are ever closer to the sources of information. Truths and half-truths abound, together with leaks, 'usually reliable sources' and all the paraphernalia of rumour.

Could a Ghanaian or Togolese news service really be any menace in such an ambiance, especially with the relatively restricted means at their disposal? One wonders today what all the fuss was about. The extraordinarily rapid diffusion of news made the old bone of contention obsolete some time ago.

Sir Geoffrey Howe took Britain out of Unesco with the words: 'We're not getting our money's worth' – words uncharacteristically ill chosen since Britain does quite well with the supply of educational materials. The fact is that Unesco is a poorer place without the absent nations.

Their discomfort in the presence of culture is well known as is their addiction to the dictatorship of the market place. It is precisely for that reason that I, holder of a British passport with a valid American visa in it, was particularly honoured to celebrate my seventieth birthday with so many of my friends at Unesco. We raised our glasses to absent friends as well.

26 April 1991

Unity from Diversity

What constitutes independence? This is a question one may well ask the agitators of history and those of today. They would certainly be in disagreement and, being agitators, their conflicts would end in disaster. Only time has mercifully kept them apart. Time and mortality.

Long ago the Italian peninsula was inhabited by a patchwork of tribes who were united by the victorious Romans. Then the barbarians confused the issue by pushing the decline of Rome to its fall. Various princes and princelings emerged from the confusion, leading eventually to a golden age of art and patronage.

With the solitary exception of the Vatican, families became almost more famous than the cities they dominated. The Medici, the Gonzaga, the d'Este and the Sforza were as renowned then as the artists they patronized are today: Michelangelo, Leonardo da Vinci, Raphael and many others.

Parts of Italy were consequently occupied by the Austrians, Sicily was dominated by the Spaniards and the disunited country became a frequent prey to foreign interference. Napoleon passed across it by force of habit. At least he knew the language. Then came the great moment when the disparate city-states and autonomous regions realized that they were all members of the same family and, under the leadership of Garibaldi and other patriotic figureheads, Italy became a kingdom, later a fascist dictatorship, later still a republic.

Today, in its wonderful and chaotic period of democracy, its adulthood, the ghosts of yesterday's divisions are not yet laid to rest. The industrious north murmurs darkly about the sun-kissed south, the rancid romanticism of the Mafia and the indolence. The south, in its turn, accuses the north of bearing the marks of Teutonic influence, of being un-Italian and dull. For the time being, the ancient regions are secure enough about their historical identities not to be clamouring for local independence at the expense of unity.

It was not without reason that Italy and Germany fought on the same side in the most recent and, one hopes, final great war. They were deprived of the sporting season of colonialism. When other, and sometimes far smaller, nations such as Portugal, the Netherlands and Belgium were adding alien jewels to their crowns, Italy and Germany were still recovering from the rigours of cohesion.

They took the scraps left after the colonial banquet and resented it deeply. Libya and Somalia on the one hand, Togo, Cameroon, Namibia, Tanzania and Samoa on the other, hardly compensated for the lack of vast territories owned even by minor powers. The doubtful theory of first come, first served drove the Italians and Germans together as outraged have-nots.

Germany had been part of the Holy Roman Empire, eventually an agglomeration of kingdoms, electorates and grand duchies, leading to its own wonderful flowering of the arts. Disunity within the same culture appears to be particularly propitious for cultural life. Now Germany is united after its punitive division. After its first almost pious days of reunion, both sides are rife with malice about each other.

While amalgamation is the order of the day in Germany, despite the internal tensions (and the devout hope of the two Koreas), elsewhere there is a desire for the Slovaks to be shot of the Czechs and the Slovenes, Croats and Serbs to be rid of each other. These peoples can more or less understand each others' languages

THE NATIONAL HERO GARIBALDIC
RECREATOR OF YUGOSLAVIA

which means that their antagonism has more to do with a profound irritation and diverse historical backgrounds than it has with incompatibility of culture.

If Yugoslavia disintegrates, will the separate republics find life easier or, as many suspect, far more difficult? Can small entities still exist in these days of necessary and desirable interdependence?

There are separatist movements even in seemingly stable countries. There are Scottish and Welsh nationalists, and Ireland has already made its point. The Basques and Catalans cherish ambitions of their own, while Bretons dream. Switzerland is an astonishing example of ethnic diversity soldered into a single unit which harbours both internecine friction and absolute solidarity against outsiders.

It will be a step backwards if there are suddenly more than 200 flags flying outside the UN building, belonging to new nations, none of which can afford to pay their dues.

A Yugoslav paper asked me how I saw the future. Perhaps Yugoslavia will disintegrate, I suggested, in the interests of the self-determination of minorities. But only until a visionary called, perhaps, Garibaldic reunites the country for precisely the same reason.

3 May 1991

Celebrating *la différence*

Having just passed three score and ten, it is infinitely rejuvenating to be celebrating a first anniversary again – that of the *European*. At first I leapt at the opportunity of expressing myself in print as a kind of release from the tensions imposed by the silent absorption of events in a world both troubled and hilarious. Today, before even re-reading myself, I enjoy the rest of the newspaper which I must confess I find increasingly interesting.

One of the principles of what those captive in it describe as the 'free world' is that competition is a necessary stimulus to even greater achievement. I am not sure that this is always true. Would Christopher Columbus really have done better if there had been a rival expedition enduring the Doldrums alongside him? Was it not enough to be a pioneer in an unknown world?

There are no exact rivals to the *European* which does not mean that there are not those, in increasing numbers, who watch its prowess with awakening interest and perhaps, at times, dismay. To be liberal is to be civilized in the view of those of a similar disposition. To enemies, it is to be negligent of high responsibility. Similarly, to be conservative appears to those, who find the appellation flattering, a stance at once reliable, forthright and sensible. Others see in it nothing but a capacity to stick in the mud for long stretches of hibernation.

It takes all sorts to make a functioning democracy, of course. And there certainly are all sorts in Europe, as any reader of the *European* knows. In Bulgaria, there are communists who say they are socialists. In Yugoslavia, there are minorities who say they are majorities and majorities who say they are treated as though they were minorities. In Britain, there are socialists who say they are socialists but behave like liberals and liberals who behave like left-wing conservatives and conservatives who seem not to notice the lack of elbow-room in their corner of the spectrum, growing more euphoric with every setback. In France, the communists insist that they are communist and are therefore becoming an endangered species.

The socialists have invaded the centre ground, the stock exchanges and big business, while right-wingers are divided against themselves, although now determined to present a single candidate for the first round of the next elections; this sounds as though they reserve the right to present two candidates for the second round if they get that far. That sounds, in advance, like a marriage of inconvenience between Gallic logic and the need for unity. In Germany, the east Germans pretend they are west Germans and the west Germans make it clear they are not east Germans, while the last Trabant car, painted a shocking pink, drives straight from the assembly line into the museum. It is evidently easier to turn over the page here, than in the Soviet Union where the confusion of ideologies is total to the extent that even the wisest and most clairvoyant commentators lay down their pens.

The most flagrant radicals seem to worship at former British Prime Minister Mrs Thatcher's galoshes, while the miners do not appear to realize how 'old hat' are strikes. The May Day celebration, the holy of holies to past generations of belligerent apparatchiks, changes to a kind of free-wheeling and formless field day in which abrasive slogans outnumber red flags and trilbies have it over the halo caps of the military. Mr Gorbachev and Mr Yeltsin appear together a little less surprisingly than might Nicholas Ridley, former British Trade and Industry Secretary, and Ken Livingstone, leader of the now defunct Greater London Council and Labour MP – or for that matter Georges Marchais, French communist leader and Charles Pasqua, former French Interior Minister – but it is still peculiar enough to confuse the pundits.

Left and right are, by now, misleading over-simplifications and hardly indicate the subtlety of

THEN & NOW

170

today's positions. Accommodation is the order of the day among the more mature nations. Violence is largely confined to those peoples with a shorter history of independence. And Europe allows friendship and cooperation between politicians as different in outlook as Edward Heath, Helmut Schmidt and Valéry Giscard d'Estaing, who would have the greatest difficulty in preserving the same relationships if they were all of the same nationality.

No wonder, in the light of this, that the cultural section of the *European* has been extended, for it is culture which is the cornerstone of amity, the prerequisite of concord. There is no continent with a greater variety than Europe of cuisines, perfumes, folk music, dance. These instinctive forms of culture, developed from historic sources, expand naturally to schools of painting, architecture, landscaping, to fashion, interior decoration and all the elements of culture which greet the eye and ear at every waking hour of the day.

It is not similarity which makes Europe what it is, but difference. It is not the average, but the outstanding. It is not the rule, it is the endless exceptions. These are the unwrapped presents of every birthday, from the first to the end of time.

10 May 1991

A Zoo is Better than War Trials

Is this to be the summer of my discontent? Certain events and tendencies are taking place in the country of my birth which I neither recognize as being typical, nor yet as being even possible. There is the suggestion, as abrupt as it seems callous, to close the London Zoo, sending some animals away and putting others to sleep by technically modern and presumably painless means.

There were, as there always are, perfectly valid reasons for such a shocking possibility. Lack of space, age of the installations and, of course, the inevitable insolvency. Oh the grim need, under this regime of shopkeepers (to quote Napoleon) for everything to pay its way, from Shakespeare and Verdi to the larger mammals.

It is curious that, at the very time that stringent measures are increasingly introduced to stop the abuses of poachers and other predators of threatened species, it is intended to do precisely what these gangsters of the bush regard as their furtive and lucrative stock-in-trade. But this time it will be done efficiently and without thought of monetary gain, merely to avoid continued monetary loss which, in the parlance of bankers, is not at all the same thing.

I expected an outcry at this announcement and there was one, of course, but not nearly on the scale which I had expected. After all, Britain is the land where our dumb friends are frequently given precedence over more loquacious friends, and in which people have from time immemorial raged about how Spaniards treat their donkeys, to say nothing of their bulls; how the

French treat their dogs and, finally, how all foreigners treat all living things that cannot answer back.

Sometimes these accusations are invalid, owing to the greater compassion which has grown around the general consciousness of ecology among peoples. But still the cries of outrage persist from those alleging to have seen ghastly abuses on their holidays. Some have even intervened with flailing parasols.

Yes, I expected more than mere expressions of sorrow at this tough decision, more than melancholy acquiescence. Of the zoo's enormous educative value there was little mention. How better to introduce children to the world which surrounds them than by showing them its inhabitants: creatures which belong to another category from humans, perhaps, but which share many attributes common to us all. These are often more directly understood by children than by adults, such as eyes one can look into and cries that are capable of interpretation.

If the conditions of the zoo's existence are outmoded and even cruel, then other conditions must be created. It is not enough just to destroy an invaluable adjunct to our knowledge and to our instincts, and treat animals the way the opera and the arts are treated, condemned to slow strangulation through inadequate funding and the application of the laws of the market to affairs of the mind and heart. If we are to be stringent about finances in these hard times of recession, then it is difficult to understand the logic of the most recent parliamentary vote in which the decision of the House of Lords was overridden in order to pursue two old residents of Great Britain for alleged war crimes. This ennobling crusade hopes to bring to justice men in their eighties for events which occurred half a century ago and in which witnesses would have to be nearly as old themselves, possessed of clear, unquestionable memories and absolute integrity. These crimes would, of necessity, have had to occur far from Britain, in parts of the world changed both in aspect and in atmosphere.

It is to be doubted if a judge, advocate and a jury, all of them very much younger than the accused, are capable of translating events into terms which have a general and precise application. If a judge were to insist on his ability to preside over such a trial, I for one would doubt his integrity. In any event, to return to the yardstick imposed by our pragmatic leaders, does the pursuit of two very old men justify the expense to the taxpayer?

THE LAST WAR CRIMINAL

Admittedly, this expense has been diminished by the death of a third old man who was originally listed as an additional target for our vindictiveness. To paraphrase Dame Agatha Christie – 'and then there were two'. Clearly, the usual slow processes of justice must at least break into a trot if these aged miscreants are not to escape mortal retribution.

All this has the dignity not so much of hitting a man when he's down, but of hitting a man when he's seated at the foot of his deathbed. There is no more money to save the lives of blameless elephants, but there are evidently sufficient funds for this demeaning and ugly procedure, a rattling of dry bones in derelict cupboards.

It is, of course, indicative of the uncertainty of events that just after President Bush had expressed hopes for a gentler America, the Gulf War broke out, giving rise to an unexpected surge of machismo, of which the immense form of General Norman Schwarzkopf became an apt trademark.

Now that the victory of high technology over bluster is more or less complete, we can perhaps turn our minds once again towards that compassion which is an essential part of the teaching of all known religions and which should be a constant force, however violent the tempests which continually buffet the human condition.

Our compassion is called for in the case of the refugees created by seemingly tidy events such as the Gulf War, as well as by local conflicts and the fury of the elements. But this continual drain on our capacity for compassion should not deprive those creatures which share existence on this planet with us, nor the wrong-headed old men now pursued by their own private Nemesis – all that is mean, reprehensible and vile in human nature.

Even to attempt to judge such men under present conditions is to lower ourselves to their level – and below – as it is to pay for their ruin in money which could be better spent elsewhere. Humans being what they are, especially in government, this last is probably the most convincing of arguments.

17 May 1991

'Madness masquerading as innocence

I have before me a fax from Rajiv Gandhi, sent in April and forwarded from the Indian embassy in Paris. For some reason, I had difficulty in answering it. Herewith part of its content:

You must have received my message regarding the postponement of the Indira Gandhi Conference 1991 on the Challenges of the 21st Century. This postponement was necessitated by the Gulf War and the economic situation in our own country. The postponed conference will now take place from 19 to 21 November, 1991 . . . I should very much like you to participate in the conference in November. I hope you will be able to schedule your commitments in such a way as to make it possible for you to attend . . .
With regards,
Yours sincerely,
Rajiv Gandhi

Well, I was already committed to playing a week in the theatre in Richmond, London, but I hesitated with my answer in case anything changed. Now it has changed. There is no need to answer. At least, not with a letter of acceptance.

I am in San Francisco at the moment, playing my one-man show. After the show I got back to the hotel at about 11pm to be greeted by my wife with the news that Rajiv had been assassinated.

My initial reaction was not so much shock as a feeling of exasperation. We were again confronted with a situ-

177

ation as horrible, as inevitable, as horribly inevitable as any Greek tragedy. Seven years ago I had accompanied his mother Indira on the campaign trail for the purpose of a television documentary. I had watched her, in all her indomitable fragility, flying from place to place in a large and noisy helicopter.

When Mrs Gandhi was in repose, and unfocused, one eye would twitch uncontrollably. When she was concentrating on a speech, the tic would disappear totally. In one day she addressed four huge crowds and opened an ordnance factory. Although addicted to peace, she was moderately belligerent as she held a small bomb in her arms. She stressed readiness for war as a guarantee of peace and independence as a prerequisite for dignified existence.

Later in the day she addressed a huge audience of hill people. The landscape was so covered by a gleaming dark crowd that it looked like the close-up photograph of a tin of caviar, extending as far as the eye could see. I remarked to her that this looked like a very good meeting. 'Well, it's a good meeting without being a great meeting,' she said. I was out of my depth and said so. 'You've got to realize,' she said, with some irritation, 'that this is one of the most under-populated areas of our country.'

The next day, while waiting for her in the garden of her administrative building under her favourite tree, we heard the sound of shots. 'Firecrackers,' remarked the Indian cameraman. 'Our people are very young at heart. When there are firecrackers left over from a festival, they use them up during the following days.' Then there was a burst of automatic rifle fire. These were no firecrackers. After seven minutes, there was another burst – evidently a settling of accounts. The garden was suddenly full of soldiers aiming at everything and nothing. We remained immobile until they had gone. Just as with Mahatma Gandhi, a peaceful

178

garden had been chosen as the scene of murder by the assassins. The Indians seem to have a predilection for places of peace in which to carry out acts of violence.

The squirrels in the garden and the vultures high up in the massive trees knew instinctively that the bullets were not meant for them and went on with their normal activities while Indira Gandhi was ripped to shreds. The aftermath was an outburst of hatred during which many Sikhs were slaughtered. I allowed ten months to pass before returning to India and attempting to finish my television portrait of Mrs Gandhi by interviewing Rajiv who could not have received me more courteously or warmly.

He may well have been less interested in politics than his younger brother Sanjay, but he never allowed it to show, more especially since Sanjay's premature death. I suggested to him that, as a pilot, he would have to consider India as the largest airliner he had ever captained. 'Yes,' he replied ruefully, 'with the woolliest of controls.'

Is it not normal and natural, I asked, that the idea of non-violence can only spring from a society which is basically violent and unstable by nature? Would the Lord Buddha have had occasion to form his opinions on human behaviour if he had not been confronted by the exact opposite of his ideal? Would Yoga and all the ascetic disciplines of the gurus have taken root in soil other than that given to waywardness and chronic untidiness? Is not the militant pacificism of Mahatma Gandhi a direct slap in the face for the follies of excessive fanaticism? Rajiv was not sure that this was true.

Now it has happened again. A bomb, possibly hidden in a garland of flowers. Once again, the madness masquerading as innocence. And where does such a murder lead? It is like trying to wound the ocean with a knife. Only an idiot can derive satisfaction from such a sterile gesture, one with no sense of tomorrow or of the day after: a cripple with a castrated mind.

24 May 1991

When Art is Hot to Handle

It is an eternal problem to know exactly what price to put on a human life. This has been debated by as eminent authorities as Genghis Khan, Torquemada, major prophets, Buddha, Stalin, Hitler and even, in a junior capacity but not lacking in opinions on the matter, Saddam Hussein. These pundits have mainly dealt in a practical sense with lives other than their own unless, of course, they belonged to that tiny minority who believed in the unequivocal sanctity of life.

Now, the case of Mr Saito is placed before us, a well-heeled and well-kimonoed captain of Japanese industry who was able to outbid all others in purchasing Renoir's famous picture *Le Moulin de la Galette* and Van Gogh's equally famous portrait of Dr Gachet for a trifling $160.6 million at New York auctions.

This was an astonishing display of the power of money which seemed to be linked for a while to the wonders of philanthropy, a splendid and by no means isolated example of responsible capitalism. He had decided to endow the Shizuoka museum with these masterpieces after his death.

He is now seventy-five years of age and a human being of any age has the right to change his mind. The whole theory of democracy is based on this premise, when you come to think of it. Well, Mr Saito has not altered his political opinions, merely his attitude towards his acquisitions. On second thoughts, he does not see why these objects, already inanimate should be allowed to survive when he himself lies cold and shrouded, awaiting disposal. Like the hissed villain in Victorian melodrama, he seems to say: 'If I can't have

181

them for all eternity, no one shall!' Have we, the public, really no recourse but hearty booing?

Mr Saito, long may he live, is the head of the Daishowa paper company, producing a highly inflammable material. Since the large majority of Japanese prefer incineration to burial, it is to be feared that the great pictures will be reduced to ashes, unlike the treasures of the Pharaohs which were to be enjoyed after death.

Now comes the news that Mr Saito has changed his mind once more, possibly surprised by the huge outcry which his purely private and personal decision has occasioned worldwide. He declares, to the general relief, that he has no intention of destroying the masterpieces.

But, of course, in a sense the harm has already been done. A man capable of changing his mind twice is capable of changing it again, and often. He has succeeded in making us nervous and apprehensive. A man of such power and experience may simply have decided not to die and, if he can pull this one off, good luck to him. Renoir and Van Gogh did it, but by more abstract methods. It is ironic to reflect that Van Gogh never succeeded in selling a single picture his whole life long and now a picture of his has been sold in an auction for $82.5 million. The descendants of those who thought his painting frankly bad now raise their voices in anguish when one of these canvasses is threatened with destruction.

Naturally, what makes this case unique is its premeditation. It gives people time to think, like a murder trial. When a lunatic attacks a picture like Rembrandt's *Night Watch* with acid, we reflect with a sigh that the world was never short of the mentally unbalanced who seek notoriety at the expense of genius. Defilers of works of art are a race apart, anti-social outlaws. They do not purchase their victims by legitimate means, in legal tender, before threatening them with extinction.

Once again, the virtual destruction of cities such as Dresden and Nuremberg could be put down to the ravages of war even if Rome and Florence escaped such treatment, presumably because Italy's industrial power was never the equal of Germany's and because Italian follies were far easier to forgive at the time. It is certain that a great deal of the obliteration of towns was wilful and could always be excused by the presence nearby of marshalling yards or some such feature; the disappearance of monuments such as Coventry Cathedral could always be justified in those untidy times by claiming that those responsible were aiming at rolling stock.

It is a virtual proof of feelings of culpability at the general lust for destruction for the sake of destruction, prevalent at the time, that today, during the Gulf War, extraordinary precautions were taken not to attack monuments of historical or religious importance. Today, there are bombs which politely enter buildings through doors and windows and do damage described as 'intelligent'.

Tomorrow perhaps, in their endless research for a spotless and impeccable form of belligerence, men of science will perfect an even more amicable type of bomb which enters a museum through the main entrance, ascertains that there is nothing remotely subversive among the exhibits, and leaves the way it entered to search out other national treasure-houses of the enemy, treacherously used as communication centres.

Yes, one thing is absolutely clear. Whereas great works of art will always be in peril during periods of upheaval, the risks to them can be minimized through the marvels of scientific invention and man's slowly dawning sense of value about his own achievements.

And yet, no scientific progress can do much to influence the whims of Mr Saito and his kind. The human mind is ever unpredictable. It is unwise to classify it as either sane or unbalanced. It can easily be both at the same time. That is its glory and its most glaring defect.

24–26 May 1991

In Defence of the Royals

So, the Queen moves majestically over the face of the erstwhile colonies like the spirit of predictability itself, a slight yet distant smile ready to accommodate every mood from adulation to hostility. The smile on the face of Prince Philip is more benign, suggesting that he can afford a readier contact with the crowd since he stands beside the footstool to the throne by right of marriage, rather than by that of birth. The British party accompanying the royals either carry with them the sullen vigilance of bodyguards or else widely beaming grins, expressing: 'Look what we have here! Isn't it a treat?'

The local reaction is what it must always have been – a mixture of gracious yet amused acceptance of another tradition, immediate surrender to its subtle choreography, or yet a refusal to allow such rituals to upset a *modus vivendi* based on the democratic principle of 'take it easy'. Curiously enough, the presence of such studied formality in their midst reduces some Americans to the posture of protesting colonists while elevating others to positions of security within the ramparts of their own traditions, by now venerable enough to stand on solid ground.

I remember being in New York a long time ago when the British journalist Malcolm Muggeridge expressed outrage at the seeming anomaly of a Royal Family in this day and age. For this piece of *lèse-majesté*, he was soundly roasted by sections of the press which have since changed their aim at times but not their stridency.

I was greeted on a popular television show by gales of caustic laughter. The host of the show asked me a good-natured question: 'What? You people call yourself a democracy? We can criticize our president, you can't criticize your Queen?' I replied: 'We can criticize our prime minister as you criticize your president, and often do. But the Queen's function in our society is different to what you imagine. She is perhaps the living embodiment of what you attribute to your flag. Can you criticize your flag?' An immediate solemnity replaced the teasing jocularity. They even seemed pained that I had brought such a sacred element into such a profane conversation. 'No,' they said soberly.

I went on to state that I had seen in *Information Please Almanac* that it was among the rules of flag lore that if Old Glory should inadvertently slip to the ground during a ceremony, it should be burned rather than be used again. Resuming the light-heartedness which is the hallmark of all talk-shows, I suggested that we were a little more civilized than they in that, if Her Majesty inadvertently stumbles, we tend to help her to her feet, even if tactile contact is frowned upon. We certainly do not condemn her to share the fate of Joan of Arc. One advantage of encounters such as the preceding one is that it enables us, inured to the presence of royalty in our midst to the point of rarely giving it a thought, to see the institution through fresh and not altogether uncritical eyes. There are those who claim that the perpetual generosity of the state even in times of penury, enabling the Queen to be by far the richest lady in the world, is wasteful and unfair. This reminds one of Henry Ford's gesture during a strike in Detroit. He said that if he were to surrender his privileges as the head of a corporation and share his fortune with his workers, they would each be $11 richer – and out of work.

Republicans consider the very institution of monarchy to be archaic. They may well be right in a sense, although I feel that Britain would be a pretty poor republic for a variety of reasons. It would be like forcing a people used to the reassurance of a tricycle suddenly to face the hazards of a bicycle. The sympathetic foreign view of the British as a somewhat ponderous, deeply fair-minded people, with a tenacious pursuit of high ideals mixed with a down-to-earth sense of the possible (a compromise which lends itself to a certain degree of hypocrisy), is due to the rigid self-censorship of the Victorian era. This time of extreme wealth and extreme poverty gave rise to both the stiff upper lip and the subservient forelock, to prudery and the belief that the Empire was God's reward for work well done.

Before the Victorians, the British had been a small, not overly rich country, aggressive by nature as well as poetic, challenging the horizons as buccaneers and the sky as lyricists and, most especially, mocking the pomp of richer monarchies with a kind of winged impertinence, expressed by phrases like 'singeing the King of Spain's beard', descriptive of a daring raid into the Spanish port of Cadiz. Today, the two natures of Britain are hopelessly entangled. The deep believers in the monarchy as an institution that foreigners would do well to emulate mingle the two strains of the contemporary British character. On the one hand, they exude the subtle conviction that only the British can truly benefit from the glories of monarchy and, on the other, they are quick on the verbal draw when heresies are in the offing. Why did Mrs Thatcher enjoy such initial popularity and such a following? For a while, she found the ideal tone in which to express this duality.

I find the Royal Family very charming people. The Queen has great intelligence and wit, when not compelled to read speeches drafted by others. Her consort is affable and bluff and Prince Charles holds views on many subjects frowned on by the royalists who believe that, like the Victorian child, he should be seen cutting tapes but not heard. Why not? It is a family of great

187

resilience, doing work which no other family in its right mind would covet. The great single moment of this American journey of the Queen was when she was enveloped in a bear-hug of tremendous warmth by a lady happily ignorant of protocol. The expression on Her Majesty's face did not change. And why should Prince Charles not express himself about architecture and anything else for that matter? This stricture is all that is palpably archaic about the institution. In fact, I am not at all sure that it does not infringe the Convention on Human Rights. At all events, it is clearly what the Americans would call 'discriminatory'; pronounced with the emphasis on 'tory' - naturally.

31 May – 2 June 1991

Conspiracies on the Menu

Washington is something else, as they say. Compared with lunch in New York, or San Francisco, or even London there is much to listen to at neighbouring tables. Let me go further. If compelled by circumstances to lunch alone and, by virtue of running behind schedule, also reduced to lunching without a book or even a magazine, there is little to prevent you overhearing conversations at neighbouring tables.

Frankly, in the cities I have mentioned, I try to avoid doing so by meditating, doing elaborate mental exercises or watching the movement of waiters and guessing at their secret thoughts about the clientele. In cities except Washington, that is.

Here, because many lunchers behave like conspirators, their voices seem to carry further and what they say is more entertaining than it would be elsewhere. First of all, it immediately becomes evident that they behave like conspirators because they are conspirators. Since virtually the only industry is government, the conversation is invariably and unswervingly confidential, but crisply audible. It is akin to the police in civilian clothes looking like policemen rather than like civilians. Secrecy is always tempted to proclaim itself.

The other day, in a distinguished small hotel, suitably refrigerated while the temperature reached 36 Celsius outside, I took my seat in a dining-room alcove close to a table with four men already toying with iced soup or paté maison. They all wore glasses which suggested, even before they opened their mouths, that they belonged to the professional class. The first one to speak did so with crisp authority, belied by the anxious

189

scanning of his eyes. 'I must be one of the few people to have read your analysis of the second amendment,' he said. The white-haired member of the quartet, the one with the juttting jaw, seemed to hope that the first speaker would continue the comment. However, nothing was forthcoming.

'How did it grab you?' he asked gruffly. There was a barely perceptible stiffening of attitudes. Anxious Eyes spoke in shrouded tones, heard with crystal clarity throughout the dining room.

'Personally, I'd be inclined to agree with you, but I think you must be out of your mind to say what you did.'

The others nodded sagely, while Jutting Jaw looked as though he might be preparing a counter-blow. It came a little later.

'You can forget anything in this goddam world,' said Jutting Jaw. 'Anything except your constituents.' They all nodded again.

One of them said: 'If you do forget them, they'll soon enough remind you.'

'Isn't that the truth, though?' cried the fourth, and they all rocked with a laughter which was surprisingly good-natured. When gravity returned with the more copious main course, they gingerly tackled the nitty-gritty.

'I feel we ought to keep an open mind as long as possible on the subject of abortion,' proposed Anxious Eyes who saw himself as a potential leader.

'You've picked yourself a tough one there,' commented Jutting Jaw.

'We're all in this, Tom. All of us. We'll all have to make up our minds sooner or later.'

'How do we go about it?' retorted Jutting Jaw doggedly, 'Consult your wives?'

'Oh Jeez, that's not the kind of thing you can discuss . . .'

'With a woman?' Big laugh.

'. . . with your wife.' No laugh.

There was a pause while they ate.

'I have a gut feeling that the sanctity of life is finally going to win out over a woman's right to be responsible for her own body.'

'I'm inclined to agree with you, but I'd hate to go out on a limb before it's necessary.'

'Who's going to tell us when it's necessary?'

'The constituents,' said the man who had brought them up before, Jutting Jaw.

'When the constituents tell you it's time, it's too late,' commented the fourth man who spoke least but most effectively.

There seemed little left for four middle-aged men to say on the subject of abortion and they devoted the coffee and cordials to less solemn banter which became inaudible for the first time, possibly because it was not worth overhearing.

They would certainly lunch with other people tomorrow, and elsewhere, and no doubt the ripples of today's encounter would spread as four different versions of it would be given, flavoured with personal condiments and spices, and news would be received of other lunches which had run concurrently with this one.

And so the business of government would be prodded on its way by fish forks and steak knives, like so much Shakespeare in modern dress.

The experience makes me reflect that no one in government can have any idea of all that is being done and undone at any given time, the cross-current, the local whirlpools and the undertow. Many people know details of this and that, without so much as a glimpse of an overview. Those at the top have only a vague notion of the details, so opaque are they when seen from above. Lunch is really the only safe bet all day long, the only

activity with a hint of consistency about it. A unique
oasis for legislators and constituents alike.

7–9 June 1991

Where the Buffalo Roam

Yesterday it was the Canadian Rockies, with the shock of cold air in the nostrils and a curious feeling that one must be recuperating from some illness to be there at all. The little town itself is full of Japanese tourists, which is understandable, since much of it is owned by their compatriots. The Japanese ladies who serve in the shops invariably say 'Sorry' before one has made a purchase, out of a conviction that they are bound to misunderstand your desires sooner or later.

This attitude merely reflects the general atmosphere of pleasantness and warmth which exists in western Canada, as it does in the Mid-West of the United States. The pervasive politeness gives an impression of balance and well-being which is perhaps a little deceptive. Under the bland smile of the surface, secret urges begin to fester as they do everywhere on this stress-ridden planet, but differently in the relative emptiness of the vast open spaces.

The reason for being there? The agreeable business of honouring a great figure of this century, Walter Cronkite, for the excellence of his long career. This was performed in a towering hotel, redolent of the architectural follies of King Ludwig of Bavaria, a symbol of the opulence of a nouveau-riche period of history in which man's relentless appetite for achievements was celebrated after a few skirmishes with vengeful Mother Nature in the belief that the victory was decisive and for all time.

The rapid changes in the weather are proof that nature is still licking her wounds on the periphery of man's penetration into the wilderness. It was pelting with rain when the guests emerged from the gala. Later, the elements abated into a state of sullen moroseness and a trickle of water was audible all night as though to give the otherwise total silence a little character. Not for long was this necessary. A woman started screaming down the hall, only two or three doors away. It was about 3am. Since I had put in a call for 5.30am I was sleeping lightly out of force of habit.

The screaming was muffled but even more strident once a door had slammed. It half opened every now and then and, for seconds at a time, the screaming threatened to become coherent, but then was choked again by the violence of the slamming door. A man, so close to me that his voice seemed to come from inside my room, yelled: 'OK girls, this is it. Square up, or I'll be along!' I had no idea what the term 'Square up' meant. It sounded like the imprecation of a boxing referee, talking to the contestants before a boxing match – 'When you hear the bell, touch gloves and square up.' Not a bit of it. It means something like 'pull yourself together'. A father, most probably, trying to strike authority into the hearts of his embattled daughters.

Around 4am another man's voice, with a foreign accent (mind you, what's foreign here?), said: 'Call the police!', repeated like a metronome, and filled with shock and horror. Occasionally, to break the monotony, it sobbed: 'I don't believe it.' Soon the corridor was filled with Royal Canadian Mounted Police in glistening raincoats, holding walkie-talkies. The hotel loudspeaker sounded loud and clear. 'There's another complaint.' 'What's it this time?' asked the policeman. 'There's a couple of guys fighting in the parking lot.' 'OK. Roger and Out.' There was no time left to sleep in this town, somnolent by day, sleepless by night. It was light well before five. An elk was eating grass under my balcony. And the freight trains had wailed during the hours of darkness like souls in torment.

A few hours later and I had a good hard look at the other smiling face of Canada, away from the ugly surprises of the hotel corridor or the unresolved battles of the parking lot. The invitation had come from the Prime Minister's office and was a soirée in Ottawa to celebrate the seventeenth birthday of his daughter Caroline. It was an event as happily relaxed as most other events in this thinly populated land of the future. In some respects, even more so.

Owing to an administrative lapse, the Governor General's limousine did not turn up. He started to walk over and was picked up halfway by his son, wearing jeans, at the wheel of his own venerable horseless carriage. Such mistakes are not brooded over. They are chuckled about.

I had already had occasion to admire Brian Mulroney's dedication to the cause of children at the Children's summit at the United Nations, of which he was one of the architects; he continues to assure us that the momentum is not lost. His interest in that particularly pressing problem is certainly inspired by the unusual serenity of his own family life. His ebullient wife, his children and he, himself, all seem to be the same age at festive moments and there can be no greater praise of their mode of life than that.

None of this has anything to do with politics. What is really remarkable about Mrs Thatcher, for instance, is not her often abrasive single-mindedness, but her disarming charm in moments of relaxation. Mr Mulroney is a man of political habits, whether indulging in witty mini-indiscretions or singing *The Wedding of the Painted Doll*. This does not prevent him from putting his family first and seeing the world through the eyes of a warm, delightful intimacy which gives him strength and resilience.

Another guest grumbled that Canada spent its time grumbling instead of indulging in what he called the 'patriotism' of the United States. I said that I liked both countries but that, as a foreigner to both, I love Canada for its lack of evident patriotism. It was too mature, I suggested, to need such reassurance.

Brian Mulroney listened to the subsequent argument with a twinkle in his eye and then produced his trump card as far as I was concerned. He revealed himself to be an assiduous reader of the *European*. I would find it difficult to cast a vote against a man of such taste and such discernment.

14–16 June 1991

Sounding Off for Sanity

Nowhere do you notice it more consistently than in New York – the veil of electronic sound which envelops us during every waking hour. Insomnia due to jet-lag in these hot and humid early summer nights forces you to take notice of what passes unnoticed during the turmoil of the day. Ingratiating little patterns of wheezing sounds punctuate the hours of darkness as though King Kong, perched on his skyscraper, was fiddling with an electronic game he had ripped from some amusement arcade.

None of the sounds are identifiable. They may come from the next room, or from beyond the horizon. They are never loud or hostile but, rather, casual. Invariably in New York there are other sounds of a more menacing and urgent nature – the police, always eager to announce their identity by fabricating their own melodrama with the Valkyrie wail of rampant sirens, often accompanied by the more grotesque bleat of the fire department's strangulated bull-horns. Intertwined with these are the less weighty and volatile hysteria of the odd ambulance, charging through the dangerous night in the aftermath of murder, suicide or mere misfortune.

In the past, the theatre had its ration of sounds. The genteel tinkle of teacups, the stirring of spoon against porcelain during matinées, or even the crackle of chocolate wrappers emanating from one of the boxes where some spoiled brat was idly dipping into a generous ration of soft centres. These sounds were natural, by which I mean unamplified. Now there is, at times, an urgent, if tiny, bell, much like an alarm clock, which is audible at some tense moment in the drama and a gentleman in the front row rises to the immense inconvenience of other spectators, caught up in the play, who must rise, one after the other, to make way for him.

The actors are invariably generous in their presumptions. It must be a great gynaecologist, summoned urgently to supervise premature labour, or something of the sort. Then there is the cellular phone. That new intruder into man's necessary and therapeutic solitude. It can be found even in the theatre or the concert-hall, its owner murmuring a litany as though in church. These are matters which cannot wait, no doubt, and which rudely proclaim themselves as having precedence over Beethoven, Shakespeare or even Lloyd Webber.

How often, during a long-distance flight, are you jolted out of a serene subservience to some favourite piece of music by the voice of the captain, proclaiming in distorted tones that you have attained a cruising altitude of 6,875 metres and that the weather at your destination is atrocious. The music resumes for a moment, after which the whole thing is repeated in gallant French or heroic Portuguese.

Just when you are reconciled to hearing the much loved last movement, there is an ominous crackle followed by the entire rigmarole repeated in Japanese. This always puzzles me because it invariably seems that far more Japanese leave the plane at the end of the journey than ever got on at the beginning. Efforts have been made to humanize this electronic Milky Way which lingers on the outskirts of our consciousness by introducing a human voice in a series of disembodied messages.

Your modern alarm clock produces a lady's voice which tells you in dehumanized terms that it is 6.15. You thought you were sharing your bed with your wife until this jarring foretaste of a ménage à trois enters your orbit with a human warmth reminiscent of matron at school.

In Los Angeles some time ago, a large automobile manufacturer kindly lent me a luxurious car for the extent of my stay. This car had an unwelcome passenger in the shape of a mincing voice tinged with viciousness and triple *entendre* which nudged you with endless comment:

'Your door is ajar.' 'Your parking lights are on.' 'Haven't you forgotten something? Your safety belt?'

In Detroit, the manufacturers of the otherwise competent car kindly invited me to dinner. I asked them whether I could hear the tapes of those rejected for the job because I just could not imagine the level of competition in which this effete fellow traveller had emerged victorious.

My hosts exchanged looks of evident embarrassment and told me the voice had since been replaced by coloured lights.

Meanwhile, despite this unusual retreat from the glacial zones of the future, other noises have been added to the list: for instance, the strangely constipated whimper of the fax machine which sounds like an old kettle undecided whether to boil or not, and the isolated scream which, at tennis matches, decides whether a service was out or not. This information is often contested by the players and, eventually, the machine is withdrawn until the next match.

So extensive is the use of these peculiar noises in the jungle in which we live that very often the telephone you rush to answer has already been answered by JR on the television screen in an umpteenth re-run of *Dallas*.

Mistakes in the identification of certain sounds not only waste time but also sap your confidence in your own judgment. And sometimes, on my encumbered desk, I hear an alarm going off under a huge pyramid of papers. I can neither stop it nor locate it and it is a tribute to the longevity of the batteries that the device still sounds years after it was first mislaid. I don't even remember what it looks like but I'd recognize its bird-call anywhere.

Now there are even machines which are supposed to invoke the noise of lapping waves, tropical rainstorms and the so-called white sound of total silence in order to help you sleep. One thing is for sure. You lie in the dark, wide awake, listening endlessly to the oppressive shout of silence, a sound so unusual that it commands your attention and banishes all hope of slumber.

21–23 June 1991

Coming Home is a Liberation

There's nothing on earth quite like a home-coming. Inanimate objects like beds or chairs or desks only have to exist to make their welcome clear. Even if it takes novelty to stimulate, familiarity helps to reassure. And especially is this so after a pilgrimage to the New World. One misses habitual newspapers over there and even to receive them one day late takes some of the morning dew off them. And then they don't travel quite convincingly, like some wines, delicious and relatively cheap in one's own garden, expensive and odd-tasting halfway round the globe.

This is less noticeable in San Francisco than it is in New York, probably because the former is a spectacular city, of human dimension, spread wilfully across what must have appeared an unpromising landscape; it has been left with absurd gradients and clattering cable cars of archaic beauty. It even has its own laconic civic humour. Confronted with what seems like a sheer precipice which you cannot see from the driving seat until your front wheels are well past the point of no return, you are nevertheless warned that you are not tumbling off into space by a diamond-shaped yellow sign upon which is written the single word, 'Hill'.

The continuous frisky sea-breeze, and the fact that it can be at once hot in the sun and icy in the shade, while most of its citizens spend at least part of every day at angles more acute than 45 degrees, give San Francisco a fiercely independent character which is more than can be said of most other large American cities. There is even far more individuality in opinions about the burning issues of the day, be they national or even international.

In only one respect does this clean and vital city resemble New York and that is in the number of vagrants who inhabit the pavements, sometimes lying down as though in the last stages of a hunger strike, with a harnessed dog, or even cat, seeming to reflect their despair, or else shuffling into your path with paper cups, ready to receive your contribution to their survival. Some of these cases must be genuine, if suitably dramatized, examples of a flagrant social inequality, but I was dismayed to be accosted within moments of my arrival in the city by a couple in tattered clothes who declared that they were in the last stages of AIDS and desperately hungry. I gave them $10. The very next morning, in precisely the same place, they renewed their cri de coeur using identical words. I asked the guy if he remembered me. He looked puzzled, as did she. I reminded him that I had given him $10 only twenty-four hours before. He extended his paper cup as though he had misunderstood what I had said.

I subsequently saw him every single morning but he had the good sense to give me a wide berth when he saw me coming. It seems churlish to believe that something as terrible as AIDS can be used unscrupulously as an additional tug at the heartstrings but I firmly believe that many of those in San Francisco who benefit from the city's reputation for sexual emancipation, by claiming that they are infected by the virus, are confidence-tricksters of the most shameless, and indeed tasteless, variety. It is curious that a in a world afflicted by the growing shadow of this particular plague, one or two cable TV stations, generally available in hotels, diffuse programmes, as explicit as they are nauseous, advertising brothels and escort services of all types, be they straight, gay or kinky.

This, only in New York as far as I could tell, adds to

the feeling of decay and imminent collapse prevalent in the streets, evidenced by the growing disrepair of the road surface, the profusion of litter and the baroque excesses of graffiti on empty buildings with shattered windows. When with old friends, you rediscover the New York you used to know. It is when you are alone that the prevailing sickness dawns on you, either when out walking, or sitting riveted, jet-lagged, in front of cable TV. And when you tell your old friends of the horrors on the little screen, they say darkly: 'Oh, that must be on cable.'

Everything has its rights, even pornography which is about as arousing as the maintenance book of a new car. It tells how it's done without imparting so much as a hint of enthusiasm about its subject. There is a glut of organs on the screen, not of the type dealt with by Dr Schweitzer in any other than his medical capacity. And the sly, come-hither looks of simulated seduction from members of all sexes, including hermaphrodites and even *hismaphrodites*!

And a series of phone numbers to ring, using unprintable words instead of numbers. Naturally, there is yet another existing right which is the right to switch off. I did this as soon as the surprise wore off, to be replaced by a dull and unutterable sadness.

In this mad penetration into the very dregs of liberty, new pressure groups will no doubt emerge, all with rights: 'Wife Beaters for a Kinder, Gentler America', or 'Child Molesters for the Sanctity of Life'. Meanwhile, I look with relief at the familiarity of my desk and the usual confusion of unanswered letters. The pilgrim is home. It's all the liberty he needs.

28–30 June 1991